MW00997675

More Christian Than African-American

One Woman's Journey to Her True Spiritual Self

Kimberly Cash Tate

Daybreak Books
An imprint of Rodale Books
Emmaus, Pennsylvania

Dedication

For my little miracles from God—
Quentin Emmanuel and Cameron Grace.
May you always know His sufficiency.

Note: Names of some people in this book have been changed to protect their privacy.

Printed in the United States of America on acid-free , recycled paper

Jacket and Interior Designer: Kristen Morgan Downey

Jacket Photographer: Mitch Mandel

Library of Congress Cataloging-in-Publication Data

Tate, Kimberly Cash.
    More Christian than African-American : one woman's journey to her true spiritual self / Kimberly Cash Tate.
        p.   cm.
    ISBN 0–87956–548–2   hardcover
    1. Tate, Kimberly Cash.   2. Christian biography—United States.
3. Afro-Americans—Biography.   I. Title.
BR1725.T22A3   1999
277.3'082'092—dc21   99–19754

Distributed to the book trade by St. Martin's Press

2   4   6   8   10   9   7   5   3   1   hardcover

Visit us on the Web at www.rodalebooks.com or call us toll-free at (800)848-4735

———— OUR PURPOSE ————

"We publish books that empower people's minds and spirits."

Acknowledgments

To my Co-Author, Whose idea gave birth to this book and Who never failed when I needed words to fill it. I love you, Lord.

To Pastor George Thomas for preaching and teaching the unadulterated Word. You lifted and He drew.

To my Christian women's network, Marilyn Parks and Bridget Thomas, for uplifting, encouraging, and supporting me from the day I voiced this vision to the day I mailed off the manuscript, and beyond. Your fervent and effectual prayers availed much.

To Daryl Tate, Tonja Tate, Christie Minga, and Krystal Williams-Oby for encouraging me in the Lord and inspiring me to keep on keepin' on.

To my church-family at St. Paul A.M.E. Church in Madison, Wisconsin, for warm and heartfelt support.

To my agent, Denise Stinson, for believing in this book and helping to make my dream come true. God blessed me with you.

To my editor, Karen Kelly, for your interest in this book, your insightful comments, and your wonderful spirit.

To my father, Earl Cash, for being a constant in my life and for loving me abundantly. And to my stepmother, Joyce Cash, for 20-plus years of open arms.

To my mother, Edna Cash, for lifelong guidance, support, and free-flowing love. Your devotion to motherhood is my model today.

To my husband, Bill Tate, for doing double duty with baby baths and bedtime stories and massaging your own insane schedule so I could get this done. When I doubted, you kept the faith; when I crept into despair, you shined a light. God sure knew what He was doing when He gave me you!

And finally . . .

"I am the Alpha and the Omega," says the Lord God (Rev. 1:8).

I begin and end these acknowledgments with the First and the Last. I thank God for His love, His many blessings, and for the opportunity to be used in this way. But most of all, I thank Him for sending us His Son, Our Lord and Savior Jesus Christ, that we might all be saved.

Contents

—⟫◆⟨—

Introduction

The Wake-Up Call

HERE IT IS. THE TRUTH. STRAIGHT UP. IT'S TIME TO STOP PLAYING around. Playing with God. All of you. Those who sleep in on Sunday mornings. *And* those of you in church. It's not about whether you fill up the pews and say a few *Amens*. It's about how you're living. By God's grace, you have a job, children, your health, a roof over your head. He's blessed you. And you take Him for granted. You don't thank Him. You don't worship Him. You don't lift a finger to serve Him. And the thought of changing your behavior to please Him is as foreign to you as His Word. But time is running out. Life is short. If you don't judge yourself now and make some changes, God will do the judging. And it might not be pretty. The nights you hung out too late to make it to church; the times you heard a good sermon and failed to live up to it; the white lies; living together out of wedlock. You're accountable for all of it.

Maybe I shouldn't be preaching. I might turn you off, make you close the book before you get well into it. I'd be safer with the simple message, "God loves you." That warm, fuzzy talk that gives you the impression you can do whatever you want and God will greet you at the pearly gates with an invitation to be His permanent guest. But that's not this book.

This book is your wake-up call. It's about saving souls. Knowing God loves you won't get you into His Kingdom. It's your actions that count. Whether you believe in Jesus Christ. Whether you live a righteous life. Opening up your eyes means dealing with some hard truths, as I've had to do. I knew God. I prayed from time to time, when a need arose. But I ignored His Word. I lived life my way, according to my own moral structure. I thought I was doing all right, too. I wasn't out acting crazy. I was responsible, an upright citizen. I worked hard in school to become a lawyer. I landed a good job and made good money. I bought a house. I got married. I had goals. I knew exactly where I was going. And I was as lost as I could be.

This book is my own personal testimony about Christian growth. It's about waking up and putting the old self to bed; it's about peeling away sin and putting on Christ; it's about listening to the Holy Spirit and tuning out the world; it's about throwing away the "gangsta" rap and cleansing with gospel music. It's about self-examination, change, sacrifice, and courage. None of it is easy; all of it is necessary. I'm still growing, trying to become a total Christian, a "24-7" Christian. More Christian than I am a woman. A lawyer. A wife. A mother. More Christian than African-American. The last has been the most difficult.

Race matters in America. It's powerful. It takes precedence. It dictates which doors will open and which minds will close. It looms over our choice of friends, neighborhoods, even church homes. It's all-encompassing. And, if you let it, it'll get in the way of your salvation.

Historically, Christianity has placed a distant second to race. Examples abound. A lot of whites were more white than Christian when they uplifted themselves, instead of God, by enslaving, killing, and dehumanizing a race of people whom they had been charged to love as they loved themselves. They were more white than Christian when they spat upon little black kids who wanted nothing more than to avail themselves of equal educational facilities. And they are more white than Christian today if they refuse to worship alongside their African-American brothers and sisters.

Black folk are guilty, too. We start salivating whenever somebody rings the Afrocentric bell—the one that sits high atop the tower in the community courtyard. It summons us in the name of blackness and alerts us to discrimination, injustice, a cause to support, a reason to unite. With rapt attention and charged emotions, we stand ready for marching orders. And our visceral reaction is to oblige.

But we can do better than a conditioned response. When we put Christ before color, we see that not every cause is worthy of support. Not every bell ringer is fit to follow. Case in point: the Million Man March. Black men from around the country were summoned to Washington, D.C., to take up their badges of responsibility and self-reliance. It was publicized as "a day of atonement" for all of the black men who had fallen short as fathers, husbands, and community leaders. Men from all economic, educational, political, and religious persuasions got caught up. Black women, too. Even Christian ministers. If they weren't there in body, they were there in spirit, uplifting the race. In caravans, buses, airplanes, and trains, African-Americans traveled to D.C. by the hundreds of thousands to answer the call. Louis Farrakhan's call.

A Muslim by trade, Farrakhan strikes at a Christian's core. Jesus, Muslims say, was solely a prophet. They call Him "Son of Mary" but deny He's the Son of God. Buy a Koran and read it for yourself. They've minimized Him, rejected Him. And anyone who calls himself a Christian, a follower of Christ, had no business following Farrakhan to D.C.

I hear you. "What did the march have to do with religion?" Everything. True religion means conforming everything we say, everything we think, everything we do, to the Word of God. There is no downtime. No lax time. Our God is a living God, on duty around the clock, watching us. Answering the call of a religious leader who believes our God is a fraud is insulting to Him. It's offensive. It's sinful. If we love Jesus, the very idea of supporting a Farrakhan-led march should have been ludicrous. Lord knows, if Farrakhan disrespected one of our loved ones, he wouldn't get support from us on anything he concocted. We wouldn't be able to separate the violation from the man. We'd wash our hands of him. That's just the way we are. When somebody tears down one we love, we get indignant.

So where's our indignation when Our Lord and Savior is violated? Our love for Him ought to be deeper than the love we feel for anyone else. He's certainly done more for us than anyone on this Earth. He suffered, bled, and died a dreadful death on the cross to save us from our sins. To save us from ourselves. *That* was our atonement. How silly it was for thousands of Christians to flock to D.C., talking about atoning for their sins. The price was paid long ago.

We have to be ready for that hour when Christ comes again. Alert. On guard. We can't afford to be sleeping. Too much is at stake. Suppose the world had ended on October 16, 1995. There's Brother Race-Conscious, part-time Christian, full-time African-American, among the crowd on the Capitol Mall. He answered the call. He knew about Farrakhan's beliefs but didn't see what they had to do with his buying a bus ticket to D.C. He didn't plan to convert to Islam. He just wanted to get his badge and be a part of history. There he is, nodding his head in his "X" hat, pumping his fist, and cheering, "You go 'head, Minister Farrakhan. Tell it. I know that's right." And it happens. In a blaze of glory, Jesus descends from the clouds to claim His faithful followers. Brother Race-Conscious screams, "Lord, Lord!" Jesus calls him over to judgment and asks, "Brother Race-Conscious, why have you followed my enemy to this place? The one who rejects me and tries to win souls from me. And why are you so swayed by his silver tongue? Have you not read the warnings I left you when last I walked the Earth?"

This is Brother's last chance for eternal life. He has to make his case. He gulps ashamedly and pleads, "Lord, I know Farrakhan doesn't believe in You, but I'm just here for his message. For real. I was just supporting the brothers. I'm not quite sure what scripture You're referring to, but I was definitely gonna be in church on Sunday. For real." Would Jesus have bought it?

Brother Race-Conscious might be a part-time Christian, but Farrakhan is no part-time Muslim. He takes his religion more seriously than most Christians. He heads the Nation of Islam. He ministers. He recruits. He's in that mode whether he's in the mosque in Chicago or in D.C., waving a flag bathed in red, black, and green. Don't get confused. He has an agenda. And we need one, too. We need to be on our job 24-7.

I know. I'm preaching again. But I can't help it. I love the Lord Jesus so much that it angers me when He's given a backseat or, worse, not asked to ride. I love Jesus so much that I will speak my mind and sing His praises even though I've risked having you close this book. But I hope you don't. I hope you read on. Walk with me through my spiritual evolution. We'll pass through the crude, primitive stages that neither look nor feel like Christianity. We'll make stops at the peaks and pitfalls that accompany growth. We'll explore the multi-layered morass of spiritual pollution that invades college, the entertainment business, and family relations. And we'll end up at a place robust and teeming with spiritual fervor. A place you won't want to leave. A place that you, too, can call your own.

Part I

Before

Chapter 1

Catholic School Girl

I BOUNDED UP THE STAIRS TWO AT A TIME TO CATCH THE PHONE, confident it would be for me. It usually was. All of my friends had the number at Daddy's, and we talked as often as teenagers do, meaning constantly. Daddy was convinced they were telepathic because the phone would begin ringing off the hook the minute I crossed his threshold and magically stop upon my departure. In the interim, they just didn't answer it.

I bore no guilt over commandeering Daddy and Joyce's sole source of outside communication. It was my lifeline. I kept my friends abreast of how to reach me, particularly in the summer, when my back-and-forth between parents fluctuated most. I hated to miss calls, to receive the late-breaking news last. So even at home, where I'd had my own phone number since ninth grade, I would liberally give out my mother's, much to her chagrin. It wasn't unusual for me to tie up both lines simultaneously, hopping from one conversation to the other, all in an effort to facilitate a constant flow of information. No one applauded louder than I when technology advanced to call waiting.

When the phone rang, I would jump up and run to a vacant room to answer it. I needed a zone of privacy in which to speak freely about teenage business. Since Daddy and Joyce were in the family room, I ran upstairs to the kitchen. When I heard the tone of voice on the other end, I froze.

"Kim?" she asked, knowing full well it was I and avoiding her customary "Hi, hon." Something was wrong, and I had a feeling that the something had to do with me. This wasn't a quivering-lip "Kim?" holding back tears caused by someone else's transgressions. It was an ominous "Kim?" squeezed between clenched teeth, a controlled anger about to erupt. Something had to be really wrong. My mother epitomized "loving" and "nurturing," and our relationship boasted those same qualities. Even when disciplining me, a responsibility she took seriously, she never blew up.

I was filled with admiration for my mother. Though she stood a petite five feet three, she towered with resilience and grit. I saw her rise in the face of challenge, even though rising meant taking a step or two backward. The day we left Daddy and became a single-parent household (when I was four years of age), we left a detached three-bedroom house that she helped buy and moved into a one-bedroom apartment. In seemingly rapid succession, though, we moved to a two-bedroom apartment; then she bought a condominium; and then, 10 years later, another house. She was about the business of taking care of home, working hard as a manager at AT&T so we wanted for nothing but forsaking company advancement if it required extended travel away from me. In my impressionable eyes, she exuded strength, determination, and always, always, control. So the sound of quiet anger bouncing off clenched teeth may have been true to form, even if the target was not.

Caught unaware, stomach knotting, I muttered, "Huh?" and braced myself for what was about to be leveled at me. And level she did. A flurry of accusations and various other unpleasantries, capping off her melee with a resounding click in my ear. Stunned, I stood for a moment in the center of the kitchen, listening to a dead phone, hoping no one would enter and intrude on my moment. I knew she was about to lose it when she hung up, preferring instead to regain her composure. She did me a favor. Still, I grew indignant over that final act. I slammed the phone into its cradle and stewed for a little while, as if I had the luxury of fuming over something so minor. But it diverted my attention from the real issue, if only for a few seconds, and it was something I could handle.

Her words had so shocked me that they had traveled from my ear directly to a waiting area in whatever part of the brain protects its owner from overload. I was allowed some time to collect myself before it spewed back at me the memory of what had just happened. But it wasn't long enough. Before I was ready to bear them, her words ripped through me again.

"I found the little note you tried to hide. I can't believe you would do this after all I've tried to teach you. You've probably been out here whoring around. I'll tell you now, if you get pregnant, I'm not going to take care of your illegitimate child. You've really disappointed me, Kim. I am just—" *Click.*

I knew exactly what letter she was talking about. I had written a close friend who had moved out of town and told her my big news of the summer. I was no longer a virgin. My mother found her return letter making reference to that fact. As I reflected on her verbal assault, I wrapped my anger around another tangent—how she acquired her ammunition.

My stashes of notes were hidden in places undetectable by respecters of privacy. I used my deepest drawer, enlisting piles of T-shirts and shorts as my shields. Nothing elaborate. No lock and key. There had been no signs of a need for such measures. I'd never caught my mother snooping nor suspected any such inclination on her part. In fact, I'd come to think that she respected my space, that I actually had rights that she held inviolable. And then this. I'd been duped, lulled into thinking there were discernible upsides to being an only child, like privacy. As I pictured her rifling through my things, I was struck by the enormity of what had happened. My space had been tainted. What else had she seen? I couldn't remember what other incriminating evidence I'd saved. I had been done in by my own pack-rat tendencies. I vowed to purge myself of all of it. My more immediate task, though, was to come up with some response. I couldn't stall any longer.

I dialed the number, and her distant "hello" told me I was expected. I hadn't much more to lose, so I went for it. "I can't believe you had the nerve to search my room. Then you hung up on me before I could say anything. If you had stopped to ask what happened, you would have found out that it was only one time, and I don't plan to do it again anytime soon. That's all I called to say. Goodbye." *Click.*

Actually, by then I had had sex twice, but I didn't want her to know *all* my business. It was sufficient that she knew I wasn't "whoring around."

I knew I was on thin ice by not giving her a chance to speak, but my "goodbye" was more than she had given me. She at least knew the click was coming. And anyway, at that moment, hanging up on my mother was the least of my worries. I still had to go home.

My mother preached abstinence until marriage from day one, citing morality as support for her principle and herself as an example that it could be done. Hardly anyone had espoused that ideal, let alone put it into practice. I simply thought her old-fashioned, a rare breed. And I had additional proof. In the decade following her divorce from Daddy, she had gone on, at most, two dates. She didn't like the idea of parading different men around me, and, besides, her trust in men had been eroded, I believe irreparably. However digestible her reasons, though, the behavior was still, well, odd. Many a concerned supporter, my paternal grandmother among them, would ask, "Does your mother have a boyfriend yet? She's too pretty to be wasting away." I would cast an "Are you serious?" look their way, and they would shake their heads, mumbling, "Unbelievable." To me, her rigid stance on premarital sex was an outgrowth of her one-of-a-kind ideals, ideals that I didn't need to necessarily adopt. But that was her position, and she stuck to it. Not "Be careful," "Get on the Pill," "Wait until you're in love." Just "Don't do it!" And I did it anyway.

I was 15 at the time, almost 16, and going on 21. That summer of 1982, everyone around me was growing up way too fast. Of those I hung around, I was about the only one who didn't have a story to tell about "the first time." And I'd certainly heard plenty of others'. In eighth grade, my friends from my old Catholic school told me about a day when six of them, three sets of couples, skipped school, met at one of their homes, dispersed into three different rooms, and had sex for the first time, all planned. That was an anomaly. I hadn't planned or thought much about sex in eighth grade, but by that summer before eleventh, curiosity was increasing.

Jeff had been my "boyfriend" off and on since seventh grade, soon after we started attending Kettering Junior High School. As teenage popularity goes, he scored high. It seemed whoever wasn't "in" enough to know him wanted to know him. Like Danny Zuko, a character in *Grease*, my favorite movie at the time, Jeff had an air that screamed self-confidence, whether he truly had it or not, and an irreverent swagger that commanded attention. That personality, coupled with unusual, light brown eyes and medium brown skin, won him the adoration of many pubescent females, myself included. When I started at Kettering, I knew just one person. So in unfamiliar surroundings, it was flattering to have Jeff, the "cool" guy, show interest in me.

By the summer of 1982, my mother and I had moved and I had enrolled in a different high school than my Kettering peers, but I was able to keep up with them. About the same time that we moved a few miles away, to Bowie, Maryland,

Daddy and Joyce moved into the Kettering neighborhood, right around the corner from Jeff. Thanks to geographic proximity and a summer spent mostly at Daddy's, Jeff and I crossed paths often, somewhere along the line agreeing to get back together.

One day he asked me to come over, his tone leaving no doubt as to what he had in mind. I should have been offended that he felt he could bring that to me. And I should have desired more innocent ways of spending my time, like asking Daddy to take me to the blockbuster movie *ET* (which I still haven't seen). But Jeff's offer intrigued me. A few days later, fully aware of expectations, I rang his doorbell. And as I walked back to Daddy's house, I had my own story to tell. It seemed a long time coming, given all I had heard, but in hindsight I was awfully young. And as I look back upon it with new eyes, I see how wrong it was, not just because my mother said so but because God said so. It had never been put to me that way. Neither my mother nor anyone else had said, "Look, if you do this, God will not be pleased." I didn't know I would be separating myself from the One I once embraced as a child. Now I know. That summer day, as surely as I walked out of Jeff's house, I had turned away from God, and far too much time would pass before I would right that and too many other wrongs.

God wasn't promoted in my house. I've been told stories over the years about prayers I used to recite at bedside and even how as a nuclear family, brief though it was, we all attended an A.M.E. church in Washington, D.C., the church in which I was baptized (and where, a few years later, Daddy and Joyce would marry). But those memories aren't mine. And whatever the rituals, they were just that. Rituals. Any effort to teach or even read the Bible, to pray as a family, to otherwise praise God, was absent at home.

The omission was born partly out of neglect but also out of the residue of pain and misunderstanding experienced by the little girl who became my mother. She had prayed to be delivered from an abusive, alcoholic father. When her circumstance lasted longer than she wanted to endure, she blamed God, assuming her plaintive cries had fallen on deaf ears. Her prayers subsided; her feelings toward God grew indifferent. And when she got out from under the thumb of abuse and grew to be successful, with her own family and home, He was not asked to dwell within it.

My knowledge as a youth of God and Jesus Christ came courtesy of Catholic school. My mother and educator father weren't overwhelmed by my public school options and believed that I'd receive a better education from the archdiocese. So, at age four, I started kindergarten at St. Margaret's in Seat Pleasant, Maryland, located down the street from our apartment and a couple of miles from the D.C. line. The goal was for me to get a good education, not necessarily a Christian one. But the steady diet of religion laid the groundwork upon which I would later build. We learned stories of the Bible, the Ten Commandments, and the Lord's Prayer. Basic Christian principles became ingrained, the overriding one being that Jesus Christ is the Son of God and Savior of the world. I would be amazed later to learn that that fact could be the point of division between Christians and non-Christian religions.

I fell in love with Jesus without trying. I was wide-eyed with awe at His greatness, His miracles, His kindness. I felt a connection, most especially after one Easter observance. St. Margaret's school and its church are located in the same building, and for special occasions, classes were adjourned early for church activities. For Easter, the tradition included a mass and a visitation of the "stations of the cross," painted depictions of the stages of Jesus' final hours, up to His death on the cross and His resurrection. By third grade, I had participated in a few such observances, but this particular year was different. The images from the pictures seemed so real, so cruel, so painful. I wondered how people could so horribly treat a Man who had been nothing but good. I lingered at each station, tears welling, disgust growing, until, as I made my way back to the pew, the tears flowed. When asked, I denied that anything was wrong, despite my runny nose and red eyes. Besides, we'd all just covered the same ground. If they couldn't understand my emotions, my verbalizing them would have been useless, even if I had known how. My heart was feeling what my mind was not yet capable of appreciating. Somehow, in some form, Jesus had made Himself known to me, and I had accepted His presence without question. Any attempt at articulating the experience would have failed miserably. I kept it to myself.

In the wake of my epiphany, I entertained thoughts of converting to Catholicism. In my mind, I'd be closer to God as a Catholic. Then I could take communion at mass, instead of looking on from the pew while my Catholic classmates climbed over me to receive the body and blood of Christ. I hated that. I wanted to take part. So my mother and I visited a priest at St. Margaret's rectory and got the rundown on what it would take for me to convert. I left dismayed. The number of classes—even that there were classes—bothered me. I had been willing to work toward the goal, but I didn't want to *feel* like I was working. I didn't reject the process; I didn't do anything. The endeavor made its way to the back burner and became a casualty of time.

I left St. Margaret's after sixth grade, two years earlier than the graduation date. Its educational value had declined in my parents' eyes, and my father knew of a new junior high school opening up, one being staffed with some of the best teachers and administrators in Prince George's County. It was time to move on, into a new and different world. Public school. No more nuns. No more uniforms. No more religion.

Neither of my parents thought of it like that . . . no more religion. It wasn't a factor in their sending me there, and it wasn't a consideration in their taking me out. Leaving didn't faze me much, though. I was intrigued by public school. Hot lunches. Gym class. Maybe I could even chew gum in class, I thought. I welcomed the change, especially when the change required a more extensive wardrobe.

My mother recognized, without my prodding, that the casual clothes I'd amassed while in Catholic school were insufficient. We embarked upon a major shopping spree, one of our favorite mother/daughter pastimes. We wasted no time on these trips. We'd get to the mall shortly after it opened and have purchases in hand by lunch as we enjoyed our other favorite pastime, eating out. Though she never left home without a budget, my mother tended toward generous more often than not. Whether I was in need of an everyday wardrobe item or a special-event outfit, she would indulge me with something extra. That pair of designer jeans that offered no better function than the Levi's found its way into the shopping bag on many an occasion. And that generosity, coupled with great taste and a penchant for quality, meant loads of surprise birthday and Christmas gifts of clothing items that I'd actually wear.

Public school brought increased independence. I joined the ranks of latchkey kids, on my own for the first time. For all of my years prior, beginning at four months of age, I'd had a caregiver in Mrs. Edwards, a sweet and highly competent woman who took her day-care job seriously. She was my mother's eyes and ears, an integral piece of our existence. When I became school age, her sky-blue Buick would daily await the school bell's ring and whisk me away to her home, where I ate, played, and watched television until my mother arrived. In junior high, the big yellow school bus replaced the blue Buick, and I assumed charge of my before- and after-school time, with rules tailored to the arrangement. I called my mother at work when I got home and refrained from having friends over without her there.

I relished my alone time. Alone for me never meant lonely. As an only child, I was quite adept at busying myself, especially if a phone was near. And music. I played albums all the time, while dancing, while singing, while doing home-work, while doing nothing. Hardly a morning or afternoon passed without aid of go-go music, Sugarhill Gang (the be-ginnings of rap music), Teena Marie, Angela Bofill, and many others.

Our neighborhood was served by Kettering Junior High, but we didn't live in the Kettering neighborhood of houses. We lived in a condominium about a mile from Kettering in Largo, an area heavy with condos, townhouses, and apart-ments. Jeff lived in a townhouse across the street from my condominium complex (before his family moved into Ket-tering), as did many of the other students. Before too long into the school year, we began hanging around the neighbor-hood at people's houses or just on the block. Friendships gelled, and for some, crushes developed, as with Jeff and me.

I had become familiar with the dynamic of crushes while at St. Margaret's. Infatuations swept across our class sometime in the fifth grade as boys began asking, with much trepidation, "Can I have a chance?" The truly anxiety-ridden would speak through a friend or pass a note asking the same question, with YES, NO, and MAYBE boxes drawn for convenience. A "yes" bought a "boyfriend," which meant silly phone conversations and shy recess encounters. A simple "I quit you" would end the relationship. I had four "boyfriends" between fifth and sixth grades, two of which I "quit" after only a day.

Junior high relationships moved a bit up the sophistica-tion scale but remained almost as harmless. We fawned over boys from afar. We talked until dawn at sleepovers about the objects of our affections, but affection itself was not what drove us. Exhilaration lay in the attraction, in daydreaming about walking the halls holding hands and, at the dream's height, sharing a French kiss. Even in our imaginations, we stayed within bounds. And if the attraction moved out of our heads and blossomed into a real relationship, the forbidden territory remained off-limits. It wasn't even broached.

By ninth grade, though, rumors surfaced that some had gone out of bounds, experimenting in the very territory others of us had deemed too foreign even for thought. These were the "bad girls." And they always seemed to be the ones who were more developed physically than we were and too "mature" for junior high boys. The bad girls were a world apart from us. We were still young and didn't mind acting it.

But the landscape changed. Somewhere between the ages of 14 and 16 lurked a vast and quickly changing set of values. Bad-girl behavior became vogue, innocence passé, "sweet 16" an oxymoron. And in talking with friends and cousins across schools, across neighborhoods, even across states, I found the phenomenon appeared universal. What was once taboo was becoming the "in" thing to do.

Submitting myself to the jurisdiction of Elizabeth Seton, a Catholic high school, should have been the perfect preventive medicine to stave off this epidemic. Not that I was seeking protection. The decision to return to Catholic school was, of course, purely academic. Still, though, the Christian by-product should have had some impact, however subtle. With the arsenal of spiritual weaponry at the school's fingertips, we should have oozed Christian discipline, despite our less-than-saintly inclinations. It could've spoon-fed our minds with regulations from on high, ones that made clear that we had no business even daydreaming about sex. Something straight and to the point like "This is okay. This isn't." But it didn't. Tuition may have included religious training, but not the kind that drives home God's brand of right and wrong. We were left strictly to home training, and since my home training didn't include a Christian component, I went without.

I often wonder if my decisions would have differed had Seton infused real-life, soul-saving instruction into the curriculum. Or if my mother had handed down a law that was attributed to God and not just herself. I might have simply crafted some self-serving loophole around the rules of even the ultimate Authority, something weak like "Times have changed since biblical days. That was then. This is now." But I'll never know. My history is fixed. In 1982, one year after returning to the sanctity of a religious institution, I abandoned my innocence. On top of that, my mother found out.

Daddy drove me home that day, oblivious to the heated exchanges that had occurred under his roof but noticeably aware of my crabby mood. I loved Daddy. He was the fun-loving parent, the one who would dare me to brave the haunted house and the steepest loop-filled roller coaster. He was the hip parent, the one with whom I shared a passion for R&B music and around whom my friends were totally chilled. He was always near, no more than 15 minutes away.

I stared out of the car window into nothingness for most of the drive, dreading the impending face-to-face. I mentally rehearsed what I would say, that is, in between Daddy's interruptions of playful banter. He challenged my sullen pout, poking me and asking, "What's your problem?" He knew I wouldn't answer but grew more amused with each exasperated "Daddy, please!" When he left me alone long enough, I contemplated game faces. There was the humble, pitiful, "I made a dumb mistake, please forgive me" look, and the defensive, eyes-rolling, "you should have minded your own business" look, the latter being my forte. I decided to play off whatever game face she chose.

I also prepared myself for a change in the way I'd be treated. Like all disobedient children, I'd be second-guessed, assumed a liar. My credibility would be nil. If I did get permission to go somewhere, I'd never make it out of the house, what with all the hours of grilling under bright lights. I'd live out the rest of high school a hermit. I could see it clearly.

We pulled into the driveway of the home my mother and I had moved into a few months before. I sighed a "See you later, Daddy" and trudged up the walkway. As I fumbled with my key in the lock, I knew she was doing some sighing of her own. Discord left a bad taste in both our mouths, and neither of us enjoyed wallowing in it. The unknown was how long it would take to quash it.

Our front door opened into the living room, which was never used, and a view of the kitchen, which was quiet. I debated where to go. My mother was downstairs in the family room. Though she couldn't see me, I knew she was watching my every move. I could have turned left, up the stairs, and retreated into my bedroom, but I dropped my bags in the living room and headed down.

My mother has never been one for histrionics. She was at her most feared when she sat silent, simmering, while I sank slowly in the quicksand of whatever shame I had created. She was in that frame when I walked into the family room. She looked up at me, raised eyebrows her only expression, wearing the hours of tears that had preceded me. With one hand, she gestured for me to sit. She had devolved to a weary calm. I sat in the wicker rattan chair diagonal to her, humbly focusing on the vacuum tread marks in the carpet. I was feeling the pull. The seconds leading up to her first communication had to be an eternity. First, an audible sigh. Then, as if grieving the loss of my better self, she stated, "I feel as if I really don't know you, as if you're a fraud."

I sank deeper, wondering, Did she really think she should know my every move? Give me a break.

She continued. "What else have you gotten into? I feel like I have to keep closer tabs on you." There it was. My prediction was right on. Constant surveillance. No social life. It was time to speak.

"Ma, I told you I haven't been running around doing anything. That was the only time." My voice trailed off as I swallowed my "fib" and added under my breath, "And you wouldn't have found out about that if you had stayed out of my stuff."

"Well," she offered, "maybe it's good that you've gotten the curiosity out of your system. This thing has just really hurt me. I . . . don't know . . . how to deal with it." Her words were breaking up. I couldn't believe she was trippin' like this. I felt part defensive and part remorseful, but totally guilty. "Well, do you have anything else to say?" she asked.

I looked around as if thinking it over seriously, then said, "Not really." She responded dismissively, "Okay, well, I know you want to go upstairs." I wanted to bolt, but instead I placed my hands on my knees slowly and made an effort at rising from my chair. I took the stairs one at a time.

Back in my room, I concluded it wasn't as bad as it could've been. She didn't even dispense any punishment to speak of. Still, she had made me feel sufficiently horrible that I resolved it would be a long time before I engaged in sex again. I didn't go so far as to say "until marriage," just "a long time," whatever that meant. Meanwhile, I was hoping our home could get back to normal. I wanted to watch our favorite shows on television with her like always, or talk in the kitchen while she cooked dinner. I spent a lot of time up in my room, listening to the radio or talking on the phone, but I didn't want to be there because I felt banished from the rest of the house.

A few hours later, at the familiar "Dinner's ready" call, I jumped up from my bed, momentarily forgetting the chill that hung in the air. I decided to wave the white flag by acting as I normally would. I walked casually into the kitchen and checked out the pots, even lifting a sample out of one. She offered peace as well, tousling my hair and asking rhetorically, "What am I gonna do with you, kiddo?" I wasn't off the hook, but we were cool again, and within a few days normalcy returned.

As it turned out, her existence didn't revolve around persecuting me for my misdeed. She allowed me my "musts" during the rest of high school—shows at the Capital Centre with my girls, dates after I turned 16, and a multitude of other events that, had I missed them, would have landed me out of the loop. We'd square off only when I skulked in the house well after the appointed hour, without having called and hoping I'd escape notice. I never did.

Surprisingly, my dates escaped persecution as well. She wasn't into making them feel uncomfortable with a slew of who, what, when, where, and why. I bore the brunt of all these inquiries in their behalf before they arrived. Typically, she would have been familiar with whoever was coming to the house. It didn't play well to ask to go somewhere with someone she'd never heard of. She had to be primed ahead of time with isolated comments like "I met this guy who's really nice. We've talked on the phone a few times already." That would get an "Oh, really?" at which time I'd fill in the name, where he lived, and what grade he was in, about the depth of information found in a fast-food application. Beyond this skeletal portrait, I didn't share a whole lot, maybe an anecdote here and there about something interesting or funny that had happened, but only if it cast a positive light on the individual. When it came down to the dirt, I was closemouthed. She never knew if we'd kissed or if he had tried something he shouldn't have. I just didn't go there. We had a close relationship, but I never forgot that she was the mother, able to judge my actions and reprimand me for them. When it came to boys, my friends, who never judged, knew more of my business than she did.

My confidantes at Seton were Lisa and Lauren, both of whom I had known since St. Margaret's. We called ourselves "Beetle, Brandy, and Boo, the Crew." I was "Brandy," named after the song I loved by the O'Jays. We were largely inseparable, especially Lisa and I. We hung out in and away from school and often stayed at each other's houses. Hardly anything happened in our lives without the others knowing. We had mechanisms in place. We talked on the phone incessantly, and during school, when classes interfered with our catch-up time, we passed notes, many of which are still in my possession. As habit would have it, I continued stashing away notes and letters even after getting busted. Since sometime late in high school, though, they've been housed in a handmade wooden box, complete with lock and key, ironically given to me by my mother.

Passing notes was an almost-daily exercise. In class and between classes, we swapped notes, always with the direction "Write back," so we could get feedback on the thoughts, news, and plans we'd written about. Our muses were highly confidential. We traded the most personal parts of our lives, our innermost thoughts. Though we sometimes sprinkled in gossip about classmates (we were, after all, an all-girl school), the topic du jour was always boys. The notes recorded a roller coaster of emotions brought about by that species, from elation at maybe having found "The One," to misery upon concluding that "all guys are dogs." But more than feelings, we shared *detail*. We wrote about whom we had talked to the night before, what was said, and how we felt about it—that is, if it was too late to call with a report when we hung up. And for me it often was. Many a night I'd talk until the wee hours of the morning to the current guy in my life, speaking softly so my mother wouldn't wake up. I'd then write Lisa a note before homeroom and give it to her when she got to school. I'd have her comments by the end of the first class. Nothing was too private. Sex and its complexities were always open for discussion.

Sex was acceptable in high school if we dated long enough. The "bad girls" were the ones who didn't, the ones we, in the black circle at least, called "freaks" behind their backs. The respectable peer standard was to wait a few months; over time, this could have resulted in quite a few partners. For me, the summer of 1982 was my only experience with sex in high school, partly because of the vow I had made that summer but also because my relationships never lasted as long as I would have liked.

I was a visionary, capable of mapping out the joint futures of myself and whomever I was dating. I'd write down his last name behind my first to test the flow and resign myself to living with syllabic incompatibility if it didn't. I was disgusting. Time and again I announced to Lisa my readiness to commit my heart and soul to the new person in my life or to trust that a castaway had mended his ways. I made repeated predictions that I could be falling in love, only to end up drowning my sorrows in song. I commiserated with L.T.D.'s "Where Did We Go Wrong" and Deniece Williams's "Silly," which I'd play over and over until I stopped feeling sorry for myself. And, at either end of the emotional spectrum, I was given to writing poetry, the tool of expression for hopeless romantics.

Lisa served as my personal advisor throughout these cycles. More often the pragmatist, she would purposely rain on my parades of optimism with friendly warnings to invest little emotional capital in the short run. And when I'd fail to heed her counsel and get burned, she participated nonetheless in the obligatory bashing of the guy who wasn't worth my time anyway.

Lisa's input in my world postdated the Jeff affair. We cemented our sisterhood in eleventh grade, a few months too late for her to have had any influence on my decision. And she certainly could have. We would have talked seriously about the issue, whether he was worthy, whether I was ready, and, at bottom, whether it was right. But "whether it was right" wouldn't have meant "morally right." It would've meant an analysis of factors to determine whether the peer respectability quotient had been satisfied: "How long have you known him? How does he act toward you? Are you in love with him? Is he a playboy?" I don't recall conversations with anyone in high school where "Is it morally right?" was touched on. Even girls who hung on to their virginity throughout high school had reasons other than morals, primarily that they, too, had not found "The One" they were looking for.

But there may have been some with real morals, Christian morals. Maybe I just wasn't close enough to them to know. Birds of a feather do flock together. Maybe those in the moral Christian circle considered my circle of friends the "bad girls." There were indeed some whom I never gravitated toward— the shy, "square" types who never sat with us at lunch and who never hung out at the same places we did. That was probably them.

There were more than 30 African-Americans in our class of almost 200, and most of us acted collectively when it came to social events. We were always down for a good time, but in order to have a good time, we had to be sure that "we" would be there in big numbers, as with the prom. Whatever committee was in charge of the planning booked the Hilton in largely white Annapolis and hired a white band as entertainment. We weren't pleased, and talk of boycott was more than idle. In the end, though, most of us decided it was our prom, too, and we would grin and bear it. Enough went to make it a fun time.

The same dynamic was at work even when a great opportunity was presented for me to go to France for spring break in 1983. My mother had said she'd get a personal loan to send me, for which I was very grateful, but I first had to be sure that "others" would be going. When Lauren, who also took French, said she could go, it was on.

But there was no question who the majority population would be at the go-go's and shows at the Capital Centre. The Capital Centre was the place. We were too young to go clubbing, but for $10 we could see four or five of our favorite music artists perform in somewhat of a controlled, safe atmosphere, at least until the "hustlers" ruined it by gang-banging and otherwise causing havoc. A few concerts came through each year, and as soon as one was advertised on the radio, the popular question among the black population would be "You goin' to the show?" The response was never "What show?" and always, barring calamity, "Yeah." The 20,000-seat arena, also home to the Washington Bullets, became more like a house party for our closest friends. The shows were "festival style," which meant the seats were first come, first served, and the entire floor was reserved for dancing. We always headed straight for the floor area beneath portal 3, and, sure enough, everyone we wanted to hook up with would be there, including my Kettering friends. We partied to New Edition, Zapp, George Clinton, Parliament Funkadelic, Cameo, Atlantic Starr, and everyone else who came to town. I didn't miss a show.

Senior week, which included the prom, brought much the same energy. The fever pitch started rising as I sent out graduation invitations and meticulously crafted my Memory Book with pictures and important (to me) news clippings from the 1983–1984 school year. I included nothing of a political bent; I wasn't yet concerned with the impact of President Reagan's policies on African-Americans, and, though I got swept up in the black pride of Jesse Jackson making a run for president, the phenomenon didn't impact me enough to include it.

I incorporated exciting stuff—the Washington Redskins making it to the Super Bowl; Georgetown winning the NCAA title; Vanessa Williams breaking the Miss America racial barrier; Michael Jackson dominating the Grammys with *Thriller;* and Eddie Murphy, the man for whom my heart beat heavily, making his meteoric rise. And I also included the sad news of Marvin Gaye's death on April 1, 1984.

My enthusiasm multiplied exponentially when my mother let me drive her red 280Z around for the whole of senior week. This was major. Ever since I'd gotten my driver's license, on the *day* I turned 16, it had been the source of much frustration. She'd cringe whenever I asked to use the car, chanting, like a broken record, that it was all she had and if anything happened to it, she couldn't get to work. I'd roll my eyes, wondering what the use was of having a fly car in the garage if I couldn't sport it. I'd maybe be allowed the privilege if the parameters of usage were tight, like going to the movies for two hours and coming right back. More often, I was relegated to Daddy's big red Chevrolet Caprice, which he didn't mind loaning out. It wasn't sporty, but it got me where I needed to go, and I didn't complain.

For senior week, though, my mother decided to rent me a car as a pregraduation accessory. I was thrilled. Then, for some reason, she offered to drive the rental herself and give me the Z. I was ecstatic. I rolled to and from school and extracurricular activities with an air of having arrived, if only temporarily. Lisa profiled alongside me in the two-seater. We soaked it for all it was worth, making appearances at as many places as we could. It was the perfect complement to a fun-filled, carefree countdown to independence.

Driving a red 280Z for a week is about what it took to get a rise out of me. Not much moved me to outward shows of excitement. I had a "whatever" mentality that earned me the tag "Miss Nonchalant." And it didn't help that my default facial expression rested at "blasé," leaving most guessing what I was feeling or whether I was feeling at all. So, on graduation morning, this genuine poker face revealed nothing of the excited and fitful sleep I'd had, kind of like Christmas Eve at age 10, when I knew something great awaited me on the other side and all that was between me and it was the night. I was eager to get going with the day, more than ready to close the Seton chapter. Not that I hated the place, but I did have some issues, racism topping the list.

In my mind, backward as it sounds, a couple of the nuns, those sworn holy beings, were racist. It manifested itself in ways that, alone, would make me sound paranoid to raise that flag but that, over time, fit right nicely. An example was algebra class with Sister Mary Patricia, a tall, broad, menacing woman who lived to instill fear in her subjects. On many a day, a white student who felt the urge to use the restroom could leave, sometimes without asking, and relieve herself. On too many a day, though, a black student's request—and it was always a request, because we wouldn't dare try to just get up and go—would be denied. One day I got sick of it. After a couple of white girls had gone, I raised my hand and asked permission, and I really did have to go. She peered down at me over her cat glasses and sneered, "No."

I stood. "But I have to go."

She ignored me, and I walked out anyway, slamming the door behind me. I didn't return. I called my mother from the pay phone, knowing they'd be calling her, too. She wasn't pleased with the way I handled the situation, but she had heard my complaints about this woman before and decided it was time for a meeting.

A few days later, the three of us had a sit-down, and my mother told her, calmly and forcefully, that she didn't appreciate the things that had gone on. That was my mother. Always professional. Always to the point. I cheered silently. Sister Mary Patricia spoke warmly, a switch from the usual, concluding that perhaps there had been a misunderstanding. After that tête-à-tête, I had no more problems with her. She seemed to even respect me. But I was still ready to get out of there.

My mother made a big deal of graduation. We had a big breakfast, I put on the new dress she had bought, and she gave me a beautiful watch with an inscription on the back. We headed to the 9:30 A.M. baccalaureate mass at the school, the prelude to the graduation ceremony that evening. The program focused on the spiritual. In caps and gowns, we sang songs glorifying the Lord, and the Catholic students took communion. I half listened to the prayers and scripture readings, which, frankly, had become rote for me. My mind was on all that had gone on within and without the school's walls. The missteps, lessons, jubilations, and regrets all were fodder for reflection. For a minute I felt sadness, not at leaving that particular institution but at closing a chapter of my life and at not knowing what to expect from the next. The scene of the next chapter, though, had long been set.

In the fall of senior year, Lisa and I had driven to the University of Maryland for Personal Decision Day, transcripts and SAT scores in hand. We walked into an office one at a time and, a few minutes later, had garnered acceptances for the fall of 1984. I had gotten through the application process in a matter of minutes and left relieved and unburdened.

That I would go to college was a given. Throughout my schooling, my mother had stressed the value of a good education so I could live comfortably and, if need be, independently, as she had. She didn't have to twist my arm. I liked school and looked forward to college. Maryland was the only school I targeted. I had visited the campus a few times when my mother was seeking a master's degree in business. She would go to the Maryland Book Exchange to purchase class materials, and I would get lost in the books and all of the college paraphernalia. I saw myself there. I was drawn to its vastness, taken in by the artfully manicured flowers that formed the *M* at the main entrance and the big white chapel on South Hill. I had ruled out the University of North Carolina, which my mother proposed, because it was too far from home. I considered for a minute a small, all-girls Catholic college in Baltimore. I even went for a guided tour. But I was tired of the all-girl environment. I wanted to see boys in class, anywhere. And I was tired, too, of the parochial nature of Catholic school. I was ready to be free.

We ended the baccalaureate mass with a rose ceremony outside in the garden around a statue of Mary, Mother of Jesus. We milled about afterward, talking to one another's parents, taking pictures, and feeling our last moments on Seton's grounds. We were wistful. Many rounds of "remember the time" rang out as we laughed and finished one another's sentences. At that moment, everything was copacetic. As much as we had lauded the coming of this day, as if we were being paroled, people were slow to leave. We weren't yet graduates, but we were one service away, and intensity was building.

The official graduation ceremony came with lots of rules. We'd actually gone to the site to practice the rules: how to march in, how to sit, how to form the line to accept the diplomas, how not to yell when a friend's name is called, and how our families shouldn't, either. Typical Catholic school stricture. The ceremony was being held at the National Shrine of the Immaculate Conception, in Northeast Washington, the largest Catholic church in the country. When I arrived for the real thing, its magnificence loomed even greater. The sea of caps and gowns set against the backdrop of its majestic architecture illuminated the grandness of the occasion. As we ascended the cascade of steps that announce the Shrine, the butterflies from the night before returned. This was it. The end. The beginning.

We formed a line in the lower level, just as we'd rehearsed, and waited for "Pomp and Circumstance" to begin the procession. The ceremony proceeded quickly. Before I knew it, I was crossing the stage to the prompt "Kimberly Ann Cash." I heard Daddy yell out. He never cared as much about decorum as my mother. I knew she was silently beaming. When the last student accepted her diploma, everyone stood in a final act of rebellion, turned her maroon-and-gold tassel from left to right, and cheered. We had rehearsed that bit on our own.

Darkness had set in by the time we recessed. Many of the goodbyes echoed earlier that day were the last heard as graduates rounded up their families, congregated briefly, and took off to their respective destinations. I saw my cousin, Craig, first and then the entourage behind him. My mother and her mother, Grandma Wade. Daddy and Joyce. Aunts and uncles. They'd all come to support me; they'd all witnessed my un-leashing. When all the hugs and well-wishes had been exchanged, my mother and I made our way to the car. Our destination was home, and the closer we got, the farther away I was from the Seton experience. Away again from religion.

The drift had already begun. For some time I had been losing a grip on my connection with Christ. It hadn't been the same since St. Margaret's. Guilt had gotten us out of the house some Sundays then. My mother's negligence had been confronted each day she dropped me off at school and saw the church alongside it. We'd go through the motions of praise every now and then to relieve her conscience. Seton was guilt-free. It had no church in which to hold mass. I had been sleeping in for years. And religion class wasn't the same at Seton. Bible stories were replaced by the philosophy of ex-istentialism. One year we even planned a fictitious wedding. The childhood love I felt for Christ had fallen victim to inat-tention and a lack of nurturing. All this while I was still sur-rounded, albeit institutionally, by religion, which was no more. Graduation had propelled me into a religion-less state. I was headed for doom and had no clue.

We pulled into the garage. I ran inside, changed my clothes, and headed to the after-party in the 280Z.

Chapter 2

Reveling

By the time I moved everything that meant anything to me into Elkton Hall, I had parted from the vow I made just two years before. I met Mark Dupree at a party graduation night and spent the better part of a lazy summer pretending we could have a meaningful relationship. He wasn't really my type—nothing about his looks distinguished him; he didn't project the self-assured, subtle arrogance I tended to favor; and he wasn't college-bound, or bound for anything as far as I could tell. But he fell for me instantly, his exuberance igniting in me a belief that it might work. Mark did wonders for my ego. He fawned over me excessively, and he was faithful, the at-your-feet, puppy-dog kind of faithful. It was sweet for a couple of months, sufficiently intoxicating that I re-entered the world of sexual relations at the ripe age of 17.

It didn't last much beyond the summer, though. Within weeks of starting my freshman year at Maryland, I began growing away from him, growing out of him. The little we had in common dissipated, and his bouts with insecurity wore on my nerves. The more he insisted I would fall for one of "those college boys," the more I wanted to. The relationship became a chore, and his sweet faithfulness turned to gross possessiveness. He'd arrive unannounced at my dorm to see if I was partying when I said I'd be studying, and wouldn't tell me about it until days later. I had the eerie feeling he was lurking about whenever I ventured out.

I knew I had to cut him off, but when I got the nerve to say it was over, he got ugly. He showed up at my first-floor dorm room, having finagled his way through two secured entrances, and demanded to know who had taken his place. After a few rounds of heated, going-nowhere debate, he pushed me, and I told him to get out. He snatched the tickets for Prince's Purple Rain tour off of my dresser, the ones I had gotten my sleep-till-noon self out of bed at 5:00 A.M. to stand in line for, and stormed out of the room. I ran after him, flagging down security at the front of the building and threatening to send him to jail. He handed over the tickets, mumbling, "Oh, you know I was just playin'." With my back already turned, I shouted, "Yeah, right," and left him alone in the night air. I never saw him again.

Lisa witnessed most of the ordeal from her vantage point atop the bunk beds. We became roommates two weeks into the school year after a university-imposed delay. We couldn't put in an advance request; policy required random assignments, then a two-week "room freeze" before the Resident Director would consider requests to move. Of all the dorms on campus, we both were assigned to Elkton Hall, an all-girls high-rise, she to the third floor, me to the first. I was paired with a spoiled white girl with a 300ZX who had gotten around the rule prohibiting freshmen from keeping their cars on campus. Within minutes of our first get-acquainted conversation, I asked if she'd be willing to move to the third floor, and she agreed to the switch.

It was a long two weeks. I'd never had to share a room with anyone, and there I was in close quarters with a stranger, a white girl, being subjected to daily blow-drying, tons of hair spray, and rock music. I made no effort to get to know her. She was an inconvenience, a two-week endurance test, not just because I preferred to room with Lisa but because I didn't want to exist in that tight a space with a white person. We could cavort in the hall or shoot the breeze in class, but not *live* together. It imposed on my blackness. I couldn't talk the way I felt most comfortable or listen to my own music without feeling inconsiderate. I needed to shut the door on white culture at the end of the day, and, instead, it was following me into my home away from home. Her presence equaled overload, and I couldn't wait to regain my equilibrium.

Truth be told, though, before seventh grade, I spent many a summer day and night with a white girl by design. Karen Zimmer and I lived in the Treetop Condominiums and camped at the community pool, she in her dirty-blond hair and me in my white bathing cap. We had no cares greater than racing each other to the farthest end of the pool and practicing single flips off the diving board until our backs no longer smacked the water. On rainy days, we played Uno or made ourselves up with grotesque amounts of makeup while profiling like queens at the vanity mirror in my bedroom. Invariably, even after a long day in each other's face, we'd beg our parents' permission to spend the night together. We'd whisper in the dark until we fell asleep, awaken, and repeat the routine.

I stopped hanging with Karen when I started junior high one year ahead of her. By the time she was old enough to join me at the bus stop, we said little more than "Hi." She huddled with her white friends, and I gathered with my black friends. We never swam together again. We never acted silly together again. We never saw the inside of each other's house again. We had discovered race, and an even greater phenomenon would have to emerge for me to get that close to a white person again.

Campus life suited me much more than it did Lisa. She routinely packed an overnight bag and hauled it home each weekend, while I found the weekend the liveliest aspect of living on the yard. The black fraternities and sororities, or "Greeks," as I came to know them, sponsored much of the formal entertainment for black students. I didn't know much about Greeks prior to college, but I received my tutorial that first semester. Things like how to pronounce the Greek letters displayed across their chests, which colors were associated with each organization, and the reputations accorded each of them.

I looked forward to parties thrown by the fraternities and sororities, and, on homecoming weekend, I witnessed my first step show. Each organization showcased itself, making grand entrances to crowd-stirring music to get the audience pumped up. They then launched into carefully rehearsed, syncopated movements, stomping their feet and waving their arms in sharp precision while chanting self-aggrandizing rhymes. The brothers of Alpha Phi Alpha stole the show that year. Of the fraternities, they had the most members on campus at the time, and the biggest following. Their parties were jam-packed, and their cheering section at the step show was unmatched. They wore black tuxedos with gold cummerbunds and worked the floor as drops of perspiration and confidence cascaded from their brows. I was smitten by their handsome control, taken in by the aura that left me wanting to know more about them. That following spring, I got my wish.

Alpha Sweethearts aid the poor souls crazy enough to abandon life as they know it and endure the physical and psychological abuse that accompanies pledging. Sweethearts place themselves at the beck and call of Sphinxmen, the pledges of Alpha Phi Alpha. Duty kicks in to high gear at about 2:00 A.M., or whenever the Big Brothers tire of putting the Sphinxmen through their paces. Sweethearts bring food, drink, and happiness to an otherwise trying day, offering Band-Aids for the mentally bruised in the form of laughter and encouragement.

I attended a Sweetheart meeting at the instance of one of the members. Only two or three people spoke, and their tone told me they regarded seriously the Sweethearts' function. One advised, "We have to be ready to go the minute they call. Who has a car? You'll have to drive to McDonald's to get the food late at night. And make sure you don't get caught by one of the Brothers, 'cause they'll take it. Take everything to Sphinxman Number Nine's room; that's where they gather. We'll have to do other things, too, whatever they need. But remember. Be discreet."

I signed up for duty, intrigued by the hush-hush nature of it all and inspired by the Alpha mystique. We organized our- selves by dorm and rotated responsibility. Somehow, though, I found myself hanging with Angie and Robin, both of whom lived in LaPlata Hall, a few high-rises over from me. Angie had a car and was willing to do anything at any time of night, especially since she was seeing one of the Sphinxmen.

My first look into the pledging process fascinated me. I'd see the Sphinxmen walking in tight formation around campus, wearing identical army-green jackets, jeans, and black army boots, faces fixed in a serious, contorted stare into space. They attracted crowds at parties as they executed the latest dance craze, the Prep, in perfect unison, while wearing black dress clothes and the same serious, unchanging expression. They were prohibited from speaking with anyone but the Big Brothers and from carrying themselves in any manner of ca- sualness. But at two in the morning, out of eye-shot of their superiors, they could relax. Angie, Robin, and I ended up in Sphinxman Number Nine's room almost nightly, and Sphinx- man Number Nine and I ended up falling for each other.

Eric Long, as he was known to the real world, brought up the rear of the line. Tall, slender, with a dark complexion, he

was hard to miss, and even harder to ignore. His playful demeanor drew others near. He somehow found humor in the
stresses of pledging, telling tales of how they'd been run amok
while acting it out for more flavor. Between pledge stories and
shuttles to and fro with food and freshly laundered Sphinx
wear, we felt a spark. I thought about him during the day and
delighted in his late-night phone calls announcing that the
Sphinxmen had been set free for the night. He counted on
me to be there, and I never let him down. For weeks we
bonded in the cover of night, stealing private conversations
and an occasional kiss. Though all around us was chaos, we
tuned in to our attraction, and all was well until time came
for the Sphinxmen to "go over," the point at which they become full-fledged Alphas. The underground connection we
had made would have to stay there. Eric had a girlfriend who
also lived in Elkton Hall, one who was waiting for him to go
over.

Nicole was a quiet, pretty young woman whom I'd often
seen in the dining halls, surrounded by a group of much
louder individuals. Her picture sat unobtrusively on his desk;
neither of us acknowledged it. I learned eventually, though,
what I'd always suspected, and we were forced to deal with
her existence upon his return to the land of the living. Eric, to
hear him tell it, was on the downside of that relationship,
taken over the edge by her lack of attentiveness to him while
he toiled on line. Though he hadn't told her so, he was
thinking of ending it and wanted me to stay in the triangle
until he sorted it all out. The "shaky ground" scenario whispered promise, a chance that maybe we could develop a real
relationship . . . an excuse to have my cake no matter who was
eating it, too.

Eric and I continued to see each other underground,
meeting in his room, because he didn't dare come to Elkton,
or at an apartment off-campus with Angie and her newly inducted Alpha. I was confronted with my "other-woman"
status whenever I saw Nicole, fending off guilt by telling my-

self, and Lisa, how stupid she was. "Eric spends all of his time with me. How could she possibly think he's being faithful?"

But being the other woman didn't suit me. In public I had to pretend Eric and I had nothing more than an Alpha/Alpha Sweetheart association, no more than what I shared with his line brothers. We barely spoke, for fear of exposing through glances what we knew to be true. I grew weary of playing the role, of being relegated to the shadows. We were growing closer all the time, physically and emotionally, and it wasn't in me to live a double life.

I tried to end it. In the first of many ultimatums, I told Eric if he couldn't make up his mind, he should leave me alone. I thought it was over. I knew he wouldn't instantly do anything, so I'd be forced to extricate myself from the mess I had a hand in creating. What good was an ultimatum, I asked myself, unless I saw it through?

But then it came. The letter. The long, heart-wrenching letter. On three pages of Alpha stationery, he exposed himself, laid bare all the nooks and crannies of his heart. He capsulized the complexity of our predicament, admitting confusion as to his next step but professing clarity about his feelings for me. He dressed his emotions in poetic phrases as he illustrated what the past few weeks had meant to him. And, in a final, adroit tug at my heart, he said he was falling in love with me. In tears, I passed the letter to Lisa. She shook her head, knowing he had me again.

We resumed relations, but as the semester neared a close, I insisted he tell Nicole the truth. If the concern was that her feelings would be hurt, as he'd been expressing, then she'd get over it. But when it became clear he had no intention of moving in the direction of honesty, I took matters into my own hands. One day, after Eric sneaked into the side door of Elkton and into my room, I had Lisa call Nicole on the hall phone and ask her to come downstairs. We all converged in the hallway. Eric's dark skin turned ashen as he stared accusingly at me and muttered, "What's going on here?" With arms folded, I returned, "You tell Nicole what's going on." He looked me dead-on and said, "What are you talking about?" I repeated my statement, and he said, "I don't know what you're talking about."

It was my turn to stare. I tried to find the weeks of bonding, the weeks of *I love yous*, behind his pitiful gaze. I thought *I* was the party privy to the truth of whom he wanted, while "poor Nicole" wallowed in ignorance. But his silence was raising doubt. I turned vindictive and produced the tear-jerking letter Eric had written me. After Nicole read it, he took her hand, said, "Come on," and left me standing in the hallway, heartbroken, embarrassed, and seething with anger.

I wrote Eric off, for a little while. When he figured I had calmed down, he offered justification for his actions, and I had the bad sense to listen. I was supposed to understand that he couldn't be put on the spot like that and that he would tell Nicole it was over in his own way and in his own time. He was sorry he had to do that to me . . . and he still loved me very much. I stood watching him as tears tumbled down his cheeks. I'd never seen a man moved to tears and unafraid to show it. I would have saved years of heartache and despair had I stood firm and kicked Eric to the curb. But I couldn't. At 18, I thought I had found real love, a love I couldn't turn my back on, for fear I might not find it again. I convinced myself we were meant to be together, and I would do all it took to make it happen.

I spent the summer of 1985 begging and borrowing my way to Baltimore, Eric's hometown. Neither of us had a car, so I made frequent use of Daddy's and sometimes made the 40-minute trip by train. I had to see him, see what he was doing. The more I saw him, the less he could see of Nicole. I got to know his mother, sisters, and brother. His youngest sister, 13-year-old Dana, resisted me at first because of her allegiance to Nicole. But I won her over, and we became tight. I stayed many nights at his house, and he stayed at Daddy's on the pullout couch. (My mother let him stay in the guest room a couple of times but then decided it was improper and put the kibosh on the arrangement.) We went to movies, Baltimore's Inner Harbor, King's Dominion—the popular amusement park in Virginia—and even my family reunion in North Carolina. We had a full summer falling deeper in love, but there was still Nicole.

The pain of that encounter at Elkton lingered. I didn't like the idea of being thought of as the fool, the side dish who miscalculated Eric's affections and got burned. In Nicole's mind, Eric had made his choice and moved on. She didn't seem to demand much time of him and, presumably, thought he was remaining faithful over the summer. I had to show her I wasn't crazy, that he did really love me and that she was the fool for believing otherwise. If she called while I was at his house, I boldly spoke in the background to let her know I was there, unaffected by Eric's resultant anger. I even called her back myself once, unbeknownst to Eric, and asked icily, "Could you please not call over here during my visits?"

Meanwhile, I confronted Eric. Often. I concluded he was a coward—afraid to make a decision and afraid to tell Nicole, or me, that it was over—and I told him so. I'd threaten to make it easy for him by leaving, and he'd say, "Maybe you're right; I don't deserve you." We'd cry and sulk over the situation, resolving nothing.

Late that summer, though, their relationship ended, I believe more due to Nicole's actions than any decisiveness on Eric's part. But it was good enough. He was mine, finally.

I didn't enter college with political dreams of advancing the black agenda. I cared about black issues, but my preoccupations were far less idealistic. And frankly, at 18, I would have been hard-pressed to articulate the specific concerns of the day. Unlike my parents, I didn't see the joy in reading 20 sections of the *Washington Post*. And as much as my mother encouraged me to watch the news, I found game shows and reruns more enticing.

So I had no burning desire to join up with the Black Student Union or the student chapter of the NAACP to affect race-related business, but I basked in the blackness I found at Maryland. We didn't have wall-to-wall culture like our brothers and sisters at historically black colleges, but, with thousands of black students, we had a small black college within a major white university. Segregation was widespread. Whites had their white fraternities and sororities; blacks had theirs. Dining halls and eateries divided along racial lines. In the dorms, whites became close friends with whites, blacks with blacks. Even in the libraries, I could spot a segregated sea of blacks among mostly white faces. And I lamented none of it. I felt strengthened by the numbers of African-Americans and enjoyed the culture we had power to import from time to time, like African-American speakers from Jesse Jackson to Attallah Shabazz to 1960s black activist Kwame Toure (f.k.a. Stokely Carmichael) to Louis Farrakhan.

During my sophomore year, I sought to further solidify myself in black life by pursuing membership in the first black incorporated sorority, Alpha Kappa Alpha Sorority. I had gone to the Delta's rush, but the AKAs impressed me by conveying the not-so-subtle message "We don't have to sell you on AKA. *You* want *us*. Work for it." I turned in my "interest letter" and, for months, willingly reduced myself into abject submission. I, along with the other "perspectives," catered to the AKAs' whims and demands. Every weekend we planned some activity—a dinner, a daiquiri party. We'd bring the food and drink, they'd partake, and then they'd commence the "bust-out" session. They'd pick us apart one by one until they had sufficiently embarrassed and belittled the lot of us. When my turn came, part of the chorus invariably started with "Stand up, Miss Cash. Miss *Alpha Queeeen*. You probably wish you were pledging Alpha, as much as you love 'em. And you better not roll your eyes." I'd stare blankly ahead, focusing on no one in particular, since even my most harmless expression was likely to be branded an attitude. "It's all a game," I'd tell myself. "Don't let them get to you."

I avoided the Student Union like the plague, especially the black section in Roy Rogers. They hung out there and looked for opportunities to humiliate us in front of the Alphas, their boyfriends, or whomever else they wanted to impress. I spent all my time with the other perspectives, the people with whom I shared a common goal. Lisa took no part in this endeavor. She moved home after freshman year, and, because others on my floor also left, I zoomed up the priority list and became one of the few sophomores to get a single room. It came in handy. After suffering through five months of process, 18 of us were voted on line, and two stayed in my room.

The actual pledging was a relief. Though it was more oppressive, we knew it was only a matter of weeks until we could sport the pink and green, AKA's trademark colors. And pledging was fun, in a narcissistic kind of way. We got a lot of attention on campus. This time *we* were the ones walking around with a stoic expression, dressed like one another in black trench coats, black pumps, and a pink hat with "Ivy" emblazoned in green on the front. Walking in line took practice. We arranged ourselves by height, which, at five feet seven, made me "Ivy Number 16," and held on tightly to one another's waists, heads held way up high. Ivy Number 1 would yell, "Ivies, march," and we'd start off on the left foot; in my head I'd hear the army chant "Left, left, left-right-left." If one person took a misstep, we all were thrown off, banging heads and driving heels into our neighbors' feet.

Technically, I couldn't talk to Eric while pledging, but I did, even crept to his room a couple of times. We were having an interesting year. He was "my man," but after all we had been through, I trusted him little. Being on line was a nightmare. I envisioned him having a cheat fest in my absence, and, as it turned out, it wasn't all in my head. A couple of weeks after I went over, someone pulled me aside and said, "I saw Eric. . . ." I dreaded those words. Whenever somebody started a sentence with, "I saw Eric . . ." or "I heard Eric . . .," I braced myself for the rest, and this was "the rest" I didn't want to hear. He was seen coming out of some girl's dorm room at night. I didn't know who she was but quickly educated myself, and the minute I laid eyes on Eric, I began my probe, starting first with a general accusation.

"So you just couldn't stay faithful while I was on line, could you?"

That elicited the usual "I don't know what you're talking about" routine. When I offered up the who and the where, his wiggle room got a little cramped. He admitted to kissing her, but nothing else.

I wanted her version and went straight to her room to get it. I told her who I was and why I was there, though I believe she knew both. She, too, declared nothing had happened. I didn't believe either of them, but since the only two with direct knowledge wouldn't admit to more, I couldn't prove my theory. The kiss was violation enough, though, and I used it like a sword to his side whenever he questioned my unyielding lack of trust.

The Alphas were the AKAs' brother fraternity, and the Sphinxmen who pledged the same semester as we did were our unofficial "line brothers." We were initiated the same night and celebrated for days, bathing ourselves from head to toe in our respective colors wherever we went. We saw one another pretty regularly, especially at our own sponsored events. But before too long, one of the neophyte Alphas, Derek Foster, fell off the bandwagon. He stopped coming to parties and, eventually, disappeared from the campus scene. The rumor was that he'd been "saved" and "born again" and had no desire to be part of the Greek world he had worked so hard for.

"Born again" and "saved" sat on the farthest ends of my periphery. I didn't even know fully what the terms meant. Derek simply became one of "those people" who stay in church all day Sunday and shun secular music. I couldn't comprehend such "extreme" behavior, let alone adopt it. I hadn't been to church in eons, except for the Sunday our Big Sisters took us to the chapel at Howard University while we were pledging. But that was for show, and I was so worn-out I fell asleep during the service.

Mine was a world apart from God. I spent the Sabbath repaying the sleep debt I'd incurred Friday and Saturday nights, then devouring a big breakfast in the dining hall and lounging around the dorm with my girls. But my distance from God was apparent in more than my failure to keep the Sabbath holy. My language was foul. Premarital sex was a way of life. And I had the tendency to treat people in an ungodly manner. I prided myself on being bold. Where others skirted issues and beat around bushes, I got to the point, feelings notwithstanding. I had no problem with confrontations or with cursing somebody out.

But bad turned to worse when a man was involved. The meanest, most unfeeling part of my soul sprang to the fore and remained on guard until the threat abated. It showed forth with Nicole, but that episode proved to be a mere preview of coming attractions. My "best" performance came opposite a Trinidadian named Alice. The leading man, of course, was Eric.

Two years after we fell into an emotionally charged romance, joy began to evade the relationship. We quarreled more and more about real and imagined wrongs. He'd been caught in one too many lies, and I challenged every excuse, every unaccounted-for stretch of time. We were hanging on by a thread, clinging to what once was, unwilling to call it quits. Enter Alice.

Alice became a thorn in my side sometime near the end of my junior year. She was 18, somewhat tall and thin, with a sharp jawline that added a toughness to her appearance. She was a recent transplant to the United States, and her hair—lots of thick ringlets—gave the impression she'd just taken a swim in the Atlantic. When I first heard rumblings of their association, Eric labeled them "just friends." But as evidence to the contrary mounted, I approached her at a campus fashion show and asked with pointed finger, "Are you seeing my boyfriend?" She responded simply, accent and all, "Eric is not your boyfriend."

A saga ensued and snowballed for months. Eric's relationship with Alice grew increasingly more serious, but he denied it to me and maintained for the longest that it was largely one-sided—her side—and that he still loved me. It was déjà vu. This time, though, I was well familiar with Eric's propensity to lie at all cost, and even tried to talk to Alice again to swap facts and pin Eric's back to the wall. But she wouldn't have it. She'd been successfully brainwashed and accused me of saying anything to keep him when I knew, allegedly, that he had told me it was over. Her naïveté unnerved me. She barely knew Eric but had decided his word was gospel, and I was the liar. Suddenly, a desire to save our relationship swept over me, not because of love but because I didn't want her to have him.

With unrelenting vigor, I haunted her. I called her on the phone a time or two to tell her what I thought of her. I'd go out of my way to walk by her and toss a nasty look or a hateful word. I'd loud-talk her around my line sisters, some of whom had no problem doubling the mischief with glances and words of their own. Alice and her friends were dubbed the "Caribbean crew," and open hostility persisted between the two camps whether I was present or not.

There were also the public scenes between Alice, Eric, and me. I found sinister pleasure in catching the two of them around campus so I could cause Eric to feel the weight of the untruths he was piling up. I'd tell him to hold my hand or to leave her and come with me, if indeed I really meant more to him. It was a sick game, driven by a need to hurt Alice and force Eric to take a stand.

The climax came in a McDonald's restaurant. The three of us met there and sat in a booth—Eric and Alice on one side, me on the other. I arranged the meeting in an effort to clear the air and rid Eric of one or the other of us. I asked him to admit that he was still pursuing a relationship with me and still proclaiming his love for me, but he wouldn't. Instead, Alice prompted him, "You love *me*, right, Eric?" In almost incoherent fashion, he managed, "Um, yeah." In disbelief, my mind flashed to freshman year in Elkton Hall. I'd been twice burned publicly by the man who claimed to love me so deeply, the one who continued to write the soul-stirring letters and cry in my arms over the thought of ending our relationship. Awkward seconds ticked as I fixated on him with a half grin that said, "You've done it this time." I stood and walked away, forcing myself to remain reserved for as long as they could see me, then drove away in tears so abundant I could barely see the road. It was over. "No matter what he says," I coached myself aloud, "it is over!"

He called that night. I knew he would. I warred with myself over whether to answer but decided he would give a doozy of an explanation that couldn't be missed, and as long as I didn't cave in, it would be okay to listen. I lifted the receiver slowly and, in my coldest voice, said, "What."

He hurriedly explained: "Kim, Alice is in the middle of a personal crisis right now, and I really have to be there for her. I don't know how long it will take, but I'm partly responsible, and I have to see it through. I know you won't wait, but you have to understand that I didn't want to say those things, I didn't want to hurt you. Kim, you know how much I love you." As his tear-filled voice trailed off, I quietly bade him a good life.

Before

I had remained sane during those final months with Eric by seeing other guys. Cutting that final thread left me completely free to roam, and I did just that with one of my line sisters, Kim Hill. A good seven or eight of us from my line formed a permanent clique, but Kim and I were joined at the hip senior year, constantly in the flow. My mother had bought me a car the summer before—an early graduation gift so I could get to an internship—and we logged some serious miles on that Hyundai. If Maryland was dead, we headed up to Howard. It was nothing to drive four hours to Virginia Beach for the Labor Day Weekend–long party, or to its neighbor, Hampton University, for homecoming. We just hopped in the car, popped in a tape—our favorite was Alexander O'Neal's *Hearsay* album—and went. We were always down for whatever. The goal was a good time, and we knew how to jump-start it. We'd go to the liquor store, buy some peach schnapps and orange juice, pour it in a McDonald's cup, and take it into the party. We drank just enough to get a buzz; we didn't want to be sloppy, just feel good.

We loved to party. We didn't hold up the wall; we danced until we were exhausted. That 1987–1988 school year, one of the big jams was a go-go song called "Da Butt," which had found popularity around the country but was especially large in D.C. Go-go music was D.C.'s baby, and, thanks to Spike Lee and his movie, *School Daze*, others were catching on to what we had been hip to for years. My relationship with Kim dipped far deeper than parties, though. We called it a sisterhood, not in reference to our sorority affiliation, which meant nothing by itself, but as an apt characterization of our connection. We gelled by the sheer force of our commonalities. Both of us had divorced parents and understood the ambivalence of loving a sometimes disappointing father. We shared the same interests and held many of the same views, down to the petty but very partisan issues that pervaded our local

42

AKA chapter. We even had similar tastes in men. We didn't go for the popular definition of a "fine" black man—light skin, green eyes, and curly hair. We wanted some color and, most of all, that "something" that triggered a spontaneous moan, that alluring confidence that screamed "SEXY." We felt it instinctively when we saw it: Cuba Gooding Jr. in *Boyz N the Hood* and Denzel Washington . . . in any movie.

But if compatibility fostered the sisterhood, trust intensified it. I never worried that Kim would divulge a word told to her in confidence, which was important given the nature of the business we shared. I was no longer passing notes about a phone conversation I had with a boy at midnight; I was telling her who I was with at midnight and what we did, down to the last detail. Neither shame nor embarrassment deterred these romps into the inner sanctum of our lives. We weren't doing anything wrong, in our opinion. Comparatively speaking, we weren't "out there." We didn't do drugs, and we turned our noses up at those women known for "giving it up" to anybody and everybody. We were just living the norm of college revelry, sowing our oats within the liberal bounds outlined by prevailing standards. I had stopped blushing long ago.

The Panhellenic Council, the University of Maryland's umbrella for black Greek organizations, sponsored an end-of-the-year picnic at the home of the Panhel President, a Que who rented a house with some of his frat brothers. With graduation a week away, it was my last hurrah as a Maryland student. Law school loomed before me. After surveying starting salaries of criminology majors and realizing my expensive tastes required more, I decided junior year that law school was the ticket. My mother promised years before to pay for my education for as far as I wanted to go, so I knew I'd have support enough to linger in the lap of career student luxury. I applied only to schools in the area, and one of my top choices,

The George Washington University, accepted me. Somehow, amid sorority life, a steady stream of extracurricular activity, and the strain of dealing with Eric, I had kept up my grades. Eric even joked once that he had done me a favor—I got my highest grade point averages during the semesters he caused the most strife.

The picnic was packed, due no doubt to the typically gorgeous spring day. My sorority sisters showed in big numbers, as did the Alphas. Eric and I were civil, as we'd been for a while. I didn't harbor open animosity. I had moved on, happy with my single life and content with the sting he felt as a result.

My life, as I regarded it then, was full. Full academically. Full socially. Full romantically. With my future mapped before me, no one questioned whether I was on the right track. Much to the contrary, I was a role model, one of few in my extended family to graduate from college, let alone move on to graduate school. I had done what was expected of me and more. I was congratulated, treated to dinners, showered with gifts and cards filled with money. And while joyous expressions of a job well-done poured my way, One with higher, very different expectations grieved.

Chapter 3

Between Black and White

By December 1989, I had grown relationship-weary, tired of whiling away my time with significant others who quickly became insignificant. After Eric, I drifted in and out of a few relationships and even tried to weather "commitment" once more. For a few months, starting with the summer before law school, I dated a guy who claimed I was his one and only. Unlike others I'd dated, Trey already was a college graduate making a good salary. I enjoyed the rides in the black BMW, the dinners out, and, though I didn't fancy him my lifelong partner, I liked being somebody's "number one" again. In primary position, I had rights to preempt phone calls, fill every inch of his weekend, and chill at his apartment when he wasn't there.

But experience told me, "Don't get too comfortable." I expected betrayal and found it hidden inside a trash can. During the Eric days, I acquired the habit of invading privacy with abandon, convinced the means were justified by the end of getting to the truth. It proved quite fruitful on many an occasion, this one included. On a day Trey left me in the apartment, I perused a couple of his dresser drawers and found pictures that looked suspect. And then I struck gold. My eyes fell upon what had once been a greeting card, ripped and scattered throughout the trash can at the corner of the dresser.

In full detective mode, I gathered the pieces, stashed them in my purse, and taped them together when I got home. My masterpiece revealed a woman's steamy recap of a lust-filled weekend at Trey's during her out-of-town visit. He had told me he was leaving town that weekend when, from the sounds of the card, he hadn't left his bedroom.

The wheels started turning, and I called North Carolina information for her number (I pieced together the envelope as well). We gabbed like old girlfriends about this man we thought was ours alone, and then I made a conference call between us and Trey. When he heard her voice and my accusation, he denied the tryst entirely, despite the evidence, and hung up. With haste, I nixed the relationship, and Kim patted me on the back for refusing to dole out a second chance.

That episode and others took their toll. I needed a break from the mind games and the disappointments. I needed to be alone, a state I had come to regard with disdain. It served as a reminder that all was not well, that my chances of having a worthwhile, long-term relationship were hopeless. But all was not well anyway; I wasn't happy biding my time with also-rans. So I decided to try "alone," linger in "alone," even enjoy "alone." That was my resolve on Friday, December 15, 1989, the night I connected with my soul mate.

I was feeling good. It was my birthday weekend. Final exams were over. One half of law school was behind me. And, within minutes of leaving my apartment, I got another boost. A local radio station, WKYS, called and congratulated me on winning a weekly singing contest. I had dialed in a few days before and recorded my a cappella rendition of "Dreamin'" by Vanessa Williams, never expecting to capture anyone's notice. But I had beaten out close to 100 other hopefuls and received an assortment of prizes.

The real value, though, was that someone had listened and judged me worthy, if only of a T-shirt and a few free albums. Not far beneath my practical, educated self lurked a dreamer. I longed to be the next Patti LaBelle, but I didn't have Miss Patti's powerhouse talent, or the guts to get an un-biased opinion as to whether I possessed even a smidgen of the gift. I couldn't give anyone the power to barricade my imagination. Seeing myself on stage, singing a heartfelt love ballad, remained viable as long as no one said I was out of my mind. This over-the-phone, you-don't-know-me, not-much-at-stake evaluation was right down my alley. *Somebody*—I didn't care if it was the disc jockey's grandchild—liked my voice, and, for one week, I sat atop the winner's circle. I glided to the car, singing "Dreamin'" the whole way.

My sorors and I had made plans to celebrate my birthday at Hogate's, a seafood restaurant on the wharf in Southwest Washington. Adjacent to the dining room, a club rocked on Friday nights, and, for a while at least, the black professional crowd descended on the place. One of my sorors, Dawn, and I were checking our coats when I saw Bill Tate walk in the front door. I waved and said to her casually, "There's your boy," and she walked over to greet him.

I don't recall that Bill and I were ever formally intro-duced, but we'd seen each other enough that only rudeness would have prevented our saying "hello." He had come to the University of Maryland in the spring of 1988 to get a Ph.D. and, because he was an Alpha, had quickly found a spot in the circle with which I had much history. But because I had moved on, from the Alphas and from Maryland, I never got to know him, Dawn did. She still traveled in that circle and sometimes teased that if she weren't dating another of the Al-phas, she'd have a mind to scoop Bill up. So I took to calling him "her boy" whenever he came near.

Dawn and I showed our I.D.s and joined the others inside. We had arrived early enough for the free happy hour. The dance floor was still empty, the air still crisp. But as more and more people made their way from work, my body tempera-ture swelled and elbow room became a prized possession.

I seized one of the coveted bar chairs that allowed one to see and be seen and began munching on buffalo wings; then Dawn whispered for me to follow her into the ladies' room. Reluctant to lose my seat, I began bargaining with one of my friends to sit there, but only until I came back. Impatient with my speed, Dawn grabbed my forearm and pulled me just inside the restroom door, exclaiming, "Girl, wait till you hear this!"

"What??"

"Bill is asking about you. Sounds like he's interested, too." Laughing, she added, "And he said you must not have a boyfriend if you're here celebrating your birthday with us. He got that right!"

Dawn advised how great a catch he would be and how great a couple we would make, then paused and waited for me to speak, as if I had the power to say, "All right, then, I'm sold. He's mine."

I wasn't in the mood to deal with Cupid. His arrow had landed in my back too many a time and left my heart cold and numb. I didn't want to go through the getting-to-know-you period, followed by the can-I-really-trust-you? period, then the maybe-I-will-trust-you phase, only to wish our paths had never crossed.

"We'll see," I tossed cynically, and went back into the club, fully expecting the so-called possibility to fade by night's end.

Some stranger had parked herself in my seat, so I stood in my cluster of friends with an admitted eye on Bill's where-abouts. Eventually, he made his way over, wished me a happy birthday, and offered to buy me a drink. As I nursed a frozen strawberry daiquiri, we nestled in the crowd, apart from our friends, and talked at length for the very first time. Conversa-tion flowed. I learned he grew up in Chicago and had spent the last few years in Dallas, first working in the school system, then obtaining a master's degree in math. He was at Maryland working on a Ph.D. in mathematics education.

My mind played it back. Black man? Math? I tripped a

little but wasn't impressed so much with his credentials as with his humility. He didn't focus on himself unless I asked the question, and even then, he muted his achievements. It was refreshing, especially given that D.C. was overrun with frauds. Some claimed to be in law school but had never seen one. Others bragged run-of-the-mill jobs into high-level executive positions and had the nerve to tote around a beeper, cell phone, and hurried demeanor to complete the charade.

"Fight the Power" broke our focus. The rap group Public Enemy had a way of mixing beats that demanded attention, and this jam was no less riveting. It filled the floor quickly, and Bill led me by hand to an inch of heated space, where we continued our dialogue a few decibels higher. I had been checking him out all along. His laid-back coolness and honey-brown complexion were definite pluses. But the dance provided a slick opportunity to check something else out. Standing shoulder to shoulder, it was tough to discern without being obvious whether he surpassed me in my two-inch heels. The verdict wouldn't carry definitive weight, but I certainly preferred that he did. When I had the gumption to dream of my perfect mate, I was never towering over him.

The crowd forced us closer still, and, unbeknownst to him, Bill Tate got two more checks in the "pro" column. His eye level rested just above mine . . . and he didn't embarrass me on the dance floor.

Bill, Dawn, and I left Hogate's at about 11:00 P.M. and walked down the block to El Torito's, where he treated us to Mexican food. Bill's friend Charles had left with a woman he'd come to Hogate's to meet, so Bill was alone and free to hang out with us. We laughed over quesadillas and enchiladas and traded stories about Maryland and the people we knew in common. We left past midnight, after a gentle nudge by our waiter, and were taken aback by the icy snowfall that had blanketed the ground. Dawn and I held fast to each of Bill's arms so our heels wouldn't fly out from under us, and Bill gallantly escorted us to our cars and scraped our covered windows. He did mine last, and afterward we exchanged numbers. The so-called possibility was awakening butterflies in my stomach.

An eyesore greeted me the next morning. From the warmth of my comforter, I could see aftereffects of the two-week exam period. Class notes on corporations and unfair trade cluttered the dining room table. Textbooks and outlines lay strewn about my hardwood floor and across the sofa. And coffee mugs with varying amounts of black goo remained where I'd last set them. It was cleanup day.

I let out a grunt, swung my legs over the side of the bed, and suddenly remembered Bill Tate. The butterflies stirred. Steadfast, I refused to allow my heart latitude to generate excitement about this new prospect. I had done it too many times to myself, only to be waylaid by reality and overcome with regret. My mind had resolved to be alone, and one evening of laughter and good conversation wasn't enough to steer me 180 degrees away from that course.

I went about my cleaning with a light step, though. When order was restored, I gathered weeks of dirty clothes, packed some clean ones, and headed to my mother's to continue my birthday weekend. We had a tradition dating back for years. Dressed in late-fall finery, we'd show up at some posh seafood restaurant, my favorite kind, and claim our reservations for two in nonsmoking. As the birthday girl, I'd have my run of the menu. Having saved myself all day for this, I'd devour a chilled shrimp appetizer, followed by a seafood bisque or chowder. The entrée would have to be jumbo shrimp– and scallop-filled, preferably broiled and served in butter. And whether room allowed or not, I would stuff down a slice of New York cheesecake. Of course, no birthday would pass without presentation of a gift. Her mommy code demanded that my mid-December birthday be special and totally set apart from the Christmas doings.

My mother had moved from Bowie, Maryland, to Herndon, Virginia, both within D.C.'s suburban hemisphere but worlds apart in commuting distance. She had been traveling more than 80 miles per day to AT&T's Oakton, Virginia, office before she was relocated a mere 8 miles away. She settled quite comfortably in a roomy three-bedroom home with three finished levels and a loft she transformed into a library.

That day, she had lifted the garage door for me so I could pull right in, and she opened the door as soon as she heard my car engine. My mother cherished the weekends I came out to visit. My company livened up the place. Radios got turned on, telephones rang at odd times of night, and movies with action she'd never watch on her own showed up on her television set. But mostly it was a chance for a mother and her grown-but-still-dependent daughter to be in each other's presence, reminisce about the same old stories, and catch up on the new.

We hugged, I hung my things up in "my" room, and we exchanged small talk while dressing for dinner. When asked whether "anything new" was happening, Bill popped into mind, and I considered mentioning him but thought better of it. I told myself to wait until I knew better if we clicked. If we didn't, I'd never mention him, and she wouldn't have to get vested in a glimmer of a possibility.

We drove to dinner in my mother's 11-year-old 280Z, sat down, and ordered our meals. I hadn't gotten farther than my cup of New England clam chowder when news of Bill slid out of my mouth.

"Well, I don't know if anything will come of it, but I met someone. . . . Well, I kinda already knew him, but we're getting to know each other better. His name is Bill."

"Oh? Tell me about this Bill."

Trying to sound blasé, I continued, "Uh, he's at Maryland in the Ph.D. program, studying math education. He's from Chicago."

Her eyes rose in approval. Education was big with her, and

a Ph.D. was real big. It said, "Smart. Disciplined. Stable." Just the kind of guy a mother would want for her only daughter.

"Good for him. Math education, huh? Good for him. When will you see him again?"

"We have plans to go out New Year's Eve. He's driving home to Chicago next week for Christmas, so I don't know if I'll see him before he leaves. But we'll see."

I changed the subject. Having already betrayed myself, I didn't want to take it too far. The less I said, the less interested I'd seem, and I could act like it didn't matter if he faded to black.

Bill called early the following week. For our first official date, we went back to the wharf for seafood, at my suggestion, then to a movie. The more we talked, the more we shared. And we talked a lot, finding common threads in our family histories, our Catholic school upbringings, and our philosophies about life. By the time his car hit the highway for Chicago, I had turned at least 90 degrees from the "alone" course and onto the path of "If it doesn't work out, then I'll be alone. . . . But I hope it works out."

New Year's Eve found me scrambling about my apartment, searching for the right outfit. It had to be nice, but not too nice. Impressive, but not so much so that he'd know I labored over it. Scads of clothes adorned my bed. Shoes and boots faced every which way, having been kicked aside in favor of the next pair. With my mirror's sanctioning, I chose a two-piece shell-pink outfit made of a soft wool. The skirt was long and straight-fitting, and I'd received enough compliments on it that I felt assured it would go over well.

Bill arrived bearing compliments of how wonderful I looked. Years later, I would don the same outfit for some other outing, and he would remark offhandedly, "Oh, is that what you're wearing? I mean, it's okay, but probably the least of my favorites." I doubt he remembered when first he saw me in it or that his taste in clothes had undergone a bit of a transformation.

We rang in the new year at festive TGI Friday's. Amid off-key party horns, colored confetti, and champagne, Bill folded his napkin, placed it slowly on the table, and said he had an announcement. To say the least, I was interested. Maybe he would produce a small black box with a shiny glass-cutting object. Stories abounded, especially in Hollywood, of marriage proposals that sprang forth in less time. Or maybe he would tell me he had a girlfriend in Timbuktu who was returning and so our whatever would be ending shortly. I twitched in my seat and waited.

"I've decided that no matter what it takes, I'm going to make you mine."

It was complete. I had done a 180. "Alone" at that point would have meant failure. Bill might not have offered marriage, but his words were about as remarkable. Some guys thrive on long-term relationships and seek to catapult a first date into immediate commitment. They smother their prey with sickening attention and marvel aloud at the wonder of finding their perfect mate . . . again. No doubt they were *someone's* perfect mate, but never mine. I figured anyone that pressed, and that available, had to have a problem.

Bill was poured from a different mold. He didn't seem pressed about anything or anybody. He was dating, but not seriously. He wanted to get married, but no time soon. He showed interest in me, but didn't fawn. And he seemed to be having a good time, but he certainly wasn't swinging from the chandeliers. I didn't know if we were headed for paradise or oblivion. And then this. Against all that he was, he laid his cards on the table. And like Cinderella, our lives changed with the stroke of midnight.

From that night forward, Bill drove daily from his apartment in Greenbelt, Maryland, to mine in Arlington, Virginia. We studied together, bought groceries together, cooked together, and relaxed together. We even went to church at St. Margaret's together on our first Easter Sunday. We had both wandered from our foundations and felt obliged to pay our respects on this, if no other, day. Bill, a baptized Catholic, took communion at the very altar I'd always wished to kneel before. Memories flooded, even of my epiphany, and I shared them for the first time with Bill. It was 15 years later, but I fumbled still with the right words to explain that feeling. And he knew. He'd felt it, too, as a child.

Our relationship soared that spring semester. We let ourselves go, daring to be silly, trusting enough to lower our guards, risking enough to love. There was no drama with him as I'd known before. I never worried about heartbreak or betrayal, insincerity or fraud. No compulsion swept over me to search his things or question his assertions. I just cozied up to calm and went with the flow of our budding romance.

After finals, we drove to Chicago. I met Bill's mother, grandmother and grandfather, and aunts and uncles, all of whom received me warmly. His grandfather, a strong family man and closet comedian, pretended to slide a wedding ring on his ring finger and pointed at Bill while looking straight at me.

"Billy, don't you let this one get away."

"I won't, E-daddy. I sure won't," he said.

Our return from Chicago marked the beginning of the summer of 1990—the summer I would try my hand at a real legal job. I worked the summer before as a research assistant for G.W.'s Government Contracts Program, but the hours were less than rigid, and we showed up for work in shorts and sandals. This was the second summer, the summer that counted.

The contest for second-summer jobs begins first year, when grades mean the most. By fall of second year, students know their approximate class rankings and whether they can add to their résumés such honors as the *George Washington Law Review,* the *George Washington Journal of International*

Law and Economics, or Moot Court Board. The right résumé means a decent shot at landing a summer associate position at a major law firm, and law school culture pushed large firms as the be-all and end-all.

When I started at G.W., the *Law Review* and *Journal* staffs were lily white, and had been for years. Legend passed from third-year black students that the last black face seen on *Law Review* was a phenomenal woman named Patricia Roberts Harris . . . back in the early 1960s. She went on to graduate first in her class and to be the first black person to hold three cabinet posts in a single administration. Her feats seemed too fantastical to match, including *Law Review*, which was minor in comparison to her other achievements.

The *Journal* goal was about as lofty. Grace Speights had last graced that office, six years before. She went on to graduate at the top of the class and land an associate position at an international law firm, one of two blacks in a D.C. office of 200.

To me, these were superstars. Beneath their strata languished class after class of minority students who, for whatever reason, weren't making these strides. But many white students weren't either. Competition was fierce. Each publication chose about 60 students. There were about 400 in each class, and most competed.

Both *Law Review* and the *Journal* sponsored their contests during spring break of first year. The competition packet, the same for both publications, consisted of a legal question and a stack of cases. Students had to read and analyze the cases, take a position in response to the legal question, and write a memorandum. Proper citation, grammar without fault, and clear, persuasive legal reasoning were key.

Law Review required a 48-hour turnaround, the *Journal* one week. And they weighted their scoring differently. *Law Review* favored grades almost exclusively, assigning 80 percent of a student's overall score to the grade point average, and 20 percent to the excellence of the written piece. The *Journal* was more balanced, assigning 60 percentage points to grades, and 40 to writing.

But a new factor was introduced during my tenure, when the school instituted the "diversity statement." Any student could submit a one-page statement about a life experience that made him or her diverse and tell how that diversity would benefit the publications. One white female student had played semiprofessional basketball in Germany for one year and wrote about that. Another had worked for a number of years before entering law school and wrote about that.

Opinions abounded around the Black Law Students Association's office as to whether we should waste our time competing. Beaten down by stories of others' rejections, some opted to spend spring break on a beach in Florida instead of a dark library filled with the untanned, anal-retentive brainiacs. I decided to go for it and pick up my packet. Worst case, I'd lose a spring break, and I didn't have big plans anyway.

I hunkered down at my mother's dining room table, away from the world, and worked voraciously for two days. No TV. No radio. I wrote, rewrote, thought, and thought about it again. And I put together my diversity statement, more than happy to speak my piece about the need for an infusion of diverse blood on both staffs.

One morning before heading out to the government contracts office, I got the call inviting me to join the *Journal* staff. I whooped and hollered. Then I called my mother, and she rejoiced, knowing that with *Journal* on my résumé, I might actually get offered a summer job in the fall.

But if *Law Review* and *Journal* competitions were fierce, the job interview process was brutal. Scores of prestigious firms from D.C. and across the country, plus a few corporations and government agencies, signed up to participate in G.W.'s on-campus interviewing season. Students received a huge bound book with information about each employer. I zeroed in on the number of minority attorneys—one or two in a large firm was, sadly, good—and I always glanced at the hiring criteria. Most firms liked the phrase "demonstrated academic excellence," which translated into "top 10 percent" for the majority of them, and "top 5 percent" for the truly pompous. I was beneath both, but I wasn't deterred. If they wanted to reject me, they could; I refused to opt my own self out of the process. We could choose 50 to whom our résumés would be sent by the school, and the potential employers had the luxury of sifting through the hundreds to glean their blue-chip candidates.

Next came the nail biting. Each day at the same appointed hour, the career development office posted on a board, for all to see, the lists of students who had been chosen for interviews. And every day, hordes of people fought to glimpse these sheets of paper, hoping their names would appear under the firms of their preference. The same names appeared across the board every day—the "stars" on *Law Review* and in the top 10 percent of the class. For them, the ritual became old hat. They looked quietly, jotted down their interview time, and moved on. The other 90 percent of us pumped a fist in the air upon discovering that someone had granted us 20 minutes of interview time.

After some initial on-campus interviews, a few callbacks, and a lot of rejection letters, I sat holding two offers in November, one from Morgan, Lewis & Bockius, and the other from Seyfarth, Shaw, Fairweather & Geraldson, both in their D.C. offices. I was torn. Morgan, Lewis had the more national reputation, and Grace Speights, who had become my mentor, practiced litigation there. But they routinely hired a large summer class, not all of whom necessarily received permanent offers at the end. Seyfarth, Shaw had small summer associate classes and a track record for extending permanent offers to all who did well. It also had a well-regarded government contracts practice. Working under a deadline, I chose Seyfarth and waited nine months to find out if I'd chosen correctly.

The Monday after returning from Chicago with Bill, I showed up early for work at Seyfarth's offices on 17th and Connecticut. I wore my black power suit, knowing on that day and every other, I'd be on stage. Much more so than the five other summer associates.

"Will she carry herself professionally? Can she articulate her ideas? Can she do excellent work?"

I knew the concerns. Being accepted by G.W., onto the *Journal*, and into the Government Contracts Program, credentials identical to many attorneys there, would not clear me of doubt. I might have slid through some affirmative action program or filled some quota undeservingly. No, they would have to scrutinize my work, and me, to determine whether I was for real and whether I had the stuff to handle a big-firm environment. On the line was a permanent offer to return upon graduation. And in an office of 65 attorneys, smack in the center of black D.C., I didn't have one black role model from whom to gain insight or receive pointers. I just relied on years of informal business training instilled by my mother, two years of in-class legal training, and common sense.

The summer proceeded well. Partners and senior associates liked my work and seemed to like me. And the firm showed us a good time. We did lunch at all the D.C.-chic places, often seated within hailing distance of popular politicos and Beltway insiders, places my student budget never knew existed.

After work, the good times kept rolling. Bill and I saw *Les Misérables* at National Theater, courtesy of a firm night out, and schmoozed at cocktail receptions at partners' swanky homes. One lived in a penthouse atop a nondescript building in Northwest Washington. The affair started on the roof, where white-gloved waiters served umbrella drinks and pretty hors d'oeuvres while we eyed a breathtaking view of the monument. Inside, we toured a condo so spacious the walk-in closets could have swallowed my entire efficiency apartment. This partner had bought two $1-million condos, knocked the walls out in between, and made this vast square footage his bachelor pad.

I felt awkward only once as the lone African-American among the Seyfarth crowd. A group of us had gone to an upscale bar after work for food and drinks, and splattered all over the television screens was the sting tape of Mayor Marion Barry feeling up Rasheeda Moore, taking hits off a crack pipe, then swearing repeatedly, "That b——— set me up," as the FBI slapped handcuffs on him. The prosecution had produced the tape that day in court and played it for the jury, and now it was being broadcast for the world to see.

When the story broke that January, it sparked much discussion in the Black Law Students office. We hashed over lots of current issues there, especially those of a legal nature. Our thin knowledge of the law fueled great debates, but opinions on this one were largely one-sided. Many, including me, blasted the mayor. The office buzzed with a flurry of comments.

"Can you believe *this* is what we've got runnin' D.C.?"

"What a disgrace!"

"You know they were out to get him. They didn't have to do all that. But man . . . he fell right into it, didn't he?"

"That's y'all's mayor. I live in Maryland."

But as I watched the tape in the bar that night, I refrained from commenting. *We* could dog the mayor behind closed doors, but my African-American rule book would not allow me to denigrate a "brother" in front of whites. So as others traded witticisms about the crack-smoking mayor, I sat silent and embarrassed, feeling the weight of my brother's foolish mistakes.

By the end of the summer, I had gotten totally caught up in the hype. I could see myself in one of the vacant associate offices, showing up for work in Ellen Tracy and Dana Buchman tailored suits, comfortably ensconced in a government contracts practice. A D.C. lawyer in a large firm making large-firm dollars. I could feel it. It was within reach. An offer wasn't a done deal, but it was mine to lose, or so I thought, and only by botching up a research assignment for one of the head honcho partners.

I would later read headlines assessing 1990 and 1991 as the worst market in years for law students. I could've written the story myself, based on my own view from the bottom.

I left Seyfarth near the end of August, unsure of my fate. That in itself signaled ruin. Most firms advised their summer associates of their fates, good or bad, before they hit the road. I was a jangle of nerves, asking Bill at every turn, "What was there left to do? They know my work. They either want me or they don't."

Bill and I flew to Dallas in the interim, where I met his father and two younger brothers. I checked my messages every few hours . . . nothing. We flew to Cancún from there and stayed three nights at the Omni. The hotel was gorgeous, the pool relaxing, and the bonding time invaluable. But peace of mind eluded me. I couldn't escape fully with uncertainty looming like a vulture over a carcass. I needed to know what the future held. I liked to be one step ahead in my planning—actually two or three—and Seyfarth was holding me up, torturously so.

The death knell sounded soon after I returned. In a form letter Seyfarth informed me, regrettably of course, that an offer could not be extended. Tears streaked my cheeks.

"I spent the summer with these people, *knew* them, and all I get is a form letter?!"

Bill looked down. There was nothing he could say. He had gotten to know them, too, and felt my disappointment.

Maria Lonzo, the only minority attorney at Seyfarth, told me later that only two offers out of six were given, one to a woman who had clerked with the firm the summer before. The market was rough, and, after some debate, the powers-that-be concluded the firm could not absorb all of us. She reassured me that my work was not the issue, that I was third in line had a third offer been approved, and that she would tell any potential employer the same thing.

I felt less than consoled. Limbo had ensnared me in its clutches and yanked my security, my future. I reeled somewhere between panic and dread, fully aware of the wall my back had been flung up against. Big firms don't interview third years in a *good* market. And if they do have space, they whip out the super-intense magnifying glass to be sure they catch all the flaws. You must be carrying not only a power résumé but also a good story to tell why you're still looking for a job third year.

Matters worsened when I called Grace Speights and received news that the bear market had bypassed Morgan, Lewis. Out of 27 summer associates, 26 got offers. "If only" chimed its two cents into an already crowded field with "second guess" and "hindsight." Grace brought temporary solace by getting me a day of interviews with Morgan, Lewis's government contracts section. They weren't sure they had space, I was told, but they'd see me.

A few weeks later, another rejection. Though I scored "tens" on my interviews, the highest possible, some expressed concern over a C that I had received in one of my contracts courses. The official party line was they didn't have a full-time spot after all.

Misery multiplied that spring semester, my last semester of law school and Bill's last semester at Maryland. For him, interviewing season was just kicking off. He had opportunities in several cities, and none of them included D.C. or its surrounding area. My mind had postponed this reality. I couldn't believe that no opportunities existed in the umpteen colleges and universities in and within driving distance of my hometown. But Bill had insisted that the only top-tier research institution in the area with a solid program in mathematics education was Maryland, which wouldn't hire its own Ph.D. students right out of school.

I pressed on. "Why do you have to be part of a *top-tier* math-ed department? You can't tell me Georgetown and G.W. aren't good schools. And you know there are lots of others."

"Kim, they're good schools. They just don't have top-ranked programs in my area."

"Sometimes we have to make sacrifices. We both like D.C., and if we want to stay here, you might have to lower your standards."

"Well, no one has published a job opening in math education around here anyway. And . . . I mean . . . it's not like you exactly have anything keeping us here."

He hated to throw it up in my face, but facts were facts. I had fallen into an abyss of jobless wonders, and with each passing month, my prospects looked bleaker and bleaker. I knew I might be able to find *something*, but the visions of grandeur I had glommed on to the summer before were long gone. The best I hoped for was to gain expertise in something elsewhere and parlay it into a lateral move down the road.

But while I wallowed in despair, Bill rolled in a sea of offers. Vanderbilt, Syracuse, and the University of Pittsburgh invited him to join their faculty ranks. And upcoming, Bill announced, would be an interview at the University of Wisconsin.

"Wisconsin? Are you for real? Isn't that the cheese state? Why in the world are you interviewing *there*? You wouldn't actually go there . . . would you?"

"I'm going because I got an interview. They're the number-one school in math-ed. Don't worry. I probably won't get an offer anyway."

The day after Bill returned from Madison, the department chair called to offer him the position. Mentors in his field, black professors, told him he'd be a fool not to start his career there, and he began to think seriously of accepting.

Bill wanted me to go with him, wherever he went, and

made it official by proposing. It was bittersweet. I wanted more than anything to be with him for the rest of my life, but not if it meant a move to Madison. It was too white. Period. I didn't want to hear about how pretty the lakes were, how wonderful an opportunity it was, or how far I needed to expand my horizons. Madison was too far left of cultural progression, and I had no intention of stepping backward in time.

My tolerance of the white collective was being pushed as it was, right at G.W. The atmosphere on the *Journal* proved stifling. I walked in the office to stares and, from the few who bothered, lukewarm greetings. In the halls, those few would pretend they'd never seen me, averting their eyes before I could form my lips to acknowledge our familiarity with one another. I had a handful of white girlfriends from first year who made it onto the *Journal*, but their warmth wasn't enough to melt the climes. I did my work, got my credits, and passed up an opportunity to compete for an editor position. Though prestigious, those positions required even more hours during the third year. I opted instead for non-résumé-building time in the BLSA office.

The last place I wanted to go was one with a larger majority of white people. I liked being somewhere that knew, understood, and had to deal with blacks. I liked being wrapped in blackness, flanked on all sides by rich culture, history, and black representation in every well-respected profession. Nurses, doctors, teachers, lawyers, bankers, chief executive officers, entrepreneurs. I didn't have to look long in any direction to see myself, and Bill's career plans threatened to remove that cloak of familiarity.

He decided to accept U.W.'s offer. My world, already upside-down, spun out of control. Stress I had never known before openly manifested itself, covering my arms with welts that itched uncontrollably. I cried. For days I just cried. Graduation was around the corner, and I didn't know where I would be working, where I would be living, or even whether I would have a relationship.

I resigned myself to losing Bill. We had been together constantly for more than a year, assured of our love and our desire to spend our lives together. By far, he was the only person who had ever truly made me happy. But he pit my blackness, my very being, against a career move to white America. I concluded maybe it wasn't meant to be if I had to give up such a great part of myself to be with him.

Advice swung in varied directions. My friends reacted as predicted.

"Madison? Where's that? I mean, is Bill trippin', or what? All the schools around here, and you're gonna tell me he can't find a job in the area? We'll never see you way out there."

I'd get defensive and regurgitate all he'd been feeding me for months. "There really aren't any opportunities here for what he wants to do. He couldn't ask for a better start to his career. . . . But it is in Madison. . . ."

My mother, who had grown quite fond of Bill, brought a different perspective.

"Well, I can't say I want to see you move that far away. But if this is who you want to spend your life with, you have to make decisions based on what's best for your future together, not just what's best for you. I know it's difficult, but he does have a wonderful opportunity before him."

I also consulted Grace Speights. Over lunch, she advised me not to reject Madison out of hand. She thought it a beautiful place to live and one where I could perhaps make a name for myself, which would be much more difficult in the glutted D.C. legal market.

Finally, I turned to God . . . with what could only loosely be termed "prayer."

"Why is this happening to me?? What did I do to deserve this?!"

My relationship with God hadn't improved much since college, but I never doubted He was ever-present, nor did I doubt His ability to fix that which seemed impossible to fix. I felt it His duty to respond in times of great need and considered this circumstance especially worthy of intervention.

He did intervene, but not in the way I had envisioned. Instead of Bill getting an instant job opportunity in D.C., I got an offer in Madison. We had agreed I would at least look, so I sent a pile of résumés to the department chair at U.W., who had graciously offered to shop them. The Thursday before Bill's graduation weekend, one week before mine, I came home to a message on my answering machine.

"Hi, this is Joni Dye, secretary to Judge Barbara Crabb of the Western District of Wisconsin. Judge Crabb would like to know if you are interested in submitting materials for a clerkship position."

She wanted to know if I could call her back. I was dialing before the message ended. The judge wanted writing samples, a transcript, and a list of references. I sent them overnight, and the next day Ms. Dye asked if I could fly to Madison for an interview. Judge Crabb was at the tail end of her interviews and wanted to make a decision right away. She was willing to come into the office that Monday, Memorial Day, to see me.

On Tuesday Judge Crabb called personally to offer me a one-year clerkship.

I didn't acknowledge or thank Him at the time, but God had blessed me in a powerful way. Students vied for federal clerkships and filled them by the end of second year. Judge Crabb had filled her other two clerkship positions the year before but had just gotten clearance for a third clerk. Without a doubt, God was at work, opening doors and implementing the plan only He knew existed. He started working as far back as the fall of my second year, when He prompted me to choose Seyfarth over Morgan, Lewis. He knew if I had gotten a permanent offer from Morgan, Lewis at the end of the summer, I would have grabbed it. So He directed me to Seyfarth, where I got nothing, which meant nothing was keeping me in D.C.

He knew if I stayed in D.C., I would have never known what was in store for me in Madison. Despite my living in sin and with my back turned to God, He lifted my deep depression and blessed me with the best job I could have gotten out of law school. It was a powerful indication that I had to go to Madison, but years would pass before I knew why.

Chapter 4

———⊰⧫⊱———

Discontent

I DETESTED MADISON. IT WAS THE WHITEST CITY I'D EVER BEEN in, and it looked to me like the citizens intended to keep it that way. It was as if over time they'd all escaped to this enclave in the north to get away from black people and would do all they could to keep us from following them. They made it as unattractive as possible. There were no black radio stations. Black movies, if they came to town, were shown in the worst theaters, the ones with hard seats and no cup holders. Finding a greeting card without a smiling white face on the cover proved an exasperating task. And black syndicated television shows without the privilege of being called *The Oprah Winfrey Show* got the worst time slots, if picked up at all by local stations.

I had landed in the twilight zone. I spoke the language, and the people looked familiar, but they had multiplied—exponentially—and stored in unknown places all the people who looked like me. Whites were everywhere, all shapes and sizes, infants to elderly, rich and poor, intelligent and not so intelligent. And then there were the clueless, so dubbed for their remarkable inability to view Madison from a black person's perspective. I had been culturally stripped at the border, and they weren't hip to the assault. I could tell. They asked incredulous questions like "Isn't Madison wonderful? Don't you just love it here?"

To whites, Madison is nothing short of choice digs. With just under 200,000 residents, a major university, and capital-city status, it's big enough to attract science and industry, the arts, and entrepreneurs, yet small enough to proclaim distance from big-city problems. Whites from elsewhere around the country, nice nuclear families with two kids and dog, move to Madison to partake of its wholesomeness. It's *so* American, *Money* magazine consistently ranks Madison in the top-10 best cities in which to live. But I didn't want American. I needed blackness. To this black woman melted lifelong in diversity, Madison might as well have been a prison sentence.

In my dreams, I could see the bars that hemmed me in. Me, a few other blacks, one or two representatives from other cultures, and thousands upon thousands of whites. I'd elbow my way through homogeneity right up to the front line, where I'd be within eye shot of home. As my nose hit the metal bars, I'd strain to get a wistful view of people enjoying all manner of cultural pleasures. All the things from which I'd been disconnected. I'd grab hold of the bars and rattle them in tearful frustration, wishing I had stayed on the other side, waiting for an opportunity to escape.

I did break out on occasion. Madison's location, near the southern border of Wisconsin, proved to be a big plus. We could drive in under three hours to Chicago's south suburbs to see Bill's family, and I learned my escape route in the process. I paid careful attention, stayed wide awake the whole ride, asked questions. Then I got a map and marked the best exits for downtown. One Saturday morning, early, I took off.

I zoomed down Interstate 90 at as high a speed as police radar would allow, feeling lighter with each passing mile. The Illinois sign welcomed me, and I started counting down the exits on the toll road. When I neared the Marengo toll plaza, my blood started pumping. I leaned forward and scanned radio stations until I got 107.5, WGCI. It wasn't crystal clear yet, but good enough. Forty miles from downtown, brothers and sisters started driving by on the highway with regularity. I almost waved with enthusiasm.

I took the Congress Parkway exit and turned left onto Michigan Avenue, eventually parking in Water Tower. As I cruised the shops on North Michigan, the intensity of the cultural bond fell upon me. I began violating all kinds of big-city codes, making eye contact with strangers and smiling at passersby. I was in my element, as close to home as I could get in the Midwest. But I couldn't stop the sun from setting. At day's end, when the car headed back north, the smile was gone. Positive feelings gone. And when static overcame WGCI at the Marengo toll, I turned off the radio and mourned all over the passing of my black existence.

For Bill, Madison wasn't all bad. He lamented the lack of diversity but could deal with cultural inconveniences for the sake of career ascension. If anything made life miserable for Bill, that "thing" would be me. It wasn't enough for me to wade in my own cesspool of negativity. I pulled Bill in with me, splashing waves of unhappiness, resentment, and bitterness whatever spiteful chance I got. Complaining became my pastime, and it moved beyond the issue of diversity. It was way too cold in Wisconsin. I couldn't watch the Redskins on Sunday. The shopping was dreadful. And I could no longer enjoy the dynamics of living in politics central.

Law school whetted my political appetite. In analyzing decades of constitutional case law, I was able to track the evolution of black rights as it moved from below-zero to halfway decent. The key to progression, I noted easily, lay in the holder of the pen, both in the legislature and, in particular, on the Supreme Court. I cherished Justice Thurgood Marshall's opinions. With brilliance he'd slam the entrenched ways of the majority population and try as best as he could to give meaning to ". . . and justice for all." I grieved when he retired, knowing President Bush would send African-Americans spiraling back in time with as conservative an appointment as his people could find. I didn't know, though, that he'd add insult to injury by making it one of our own with the nomination of Clarence Thomas.

I thought it couldn't get any more bizarre . . . until Anita Hill stepped forward and the nation became embroiled in an African-American "he said/she said." It pained me to watch "our" dirty laundry being aired on the Senate floor, but I was behind Anita Hill all the way. I believed her and watched every minute of coverage I could find on television.

But I still wanted to be there, in D.C., in the thick of it. It was the fall of 1991, and we'd been in Madison only since the first of August. I could imagine vividly what I was missing—top-rate local news coverage, both print and media, as well as the nuggets of information floating on the inside-the-beltway grapevine. Meanwhile, I was in no-man's-land, watching CNN with the rest of the country, way outside the loop. The political event gave me one more grievance to tick off and yet another opportunity to ask, "And, anyway, how long did you say we had to be here?"

Bill made a promise before we left D.C. that we wouldn't be in Madison more than a couple of years. I clung to it like a lifeline and reminded him of it whenever he hinted at placing down a root.

"I wonder what the quality of the grade schools is here," he said early on.

I pounced. "I don't know why, 'cause we won't be here long enough for it to matter. I will *not* do any child of mine the disservice of raising him or her in this lily-white place. It's not fair. We both were raised in the privilege of diversity, and I want our children to be as well."

Fixing my mind on an up-and-out game plan gave me comfort, like a lollipop to a screaming toddler. And that lol-

lipop came in real handy during January and February. Having
no fondness for Madison to begin with, winter only threw salt
in my aggravated wound. I'd trudge through piles of dirty
snow in below-zero wind chills, one hand holding an errant
scarf over my mouth, the other seeking shelter in my woolen
pocket, and the mantra would surface.

"It won't be long. It won't be long. One or two more win-
ters. It won't be long."

On wintry days, I found pleasure in tall mugs of hot cocoa
doused with crazy amounts of whipped cream. Judge Crabb's
chambers were about as soothing. Simply stepping inside for
work each day coated my frustrations. The environment was
comfortable, untroubled. Joni, the judge's right hand of more
than 15 years, set the tone. Sitting at her station in the outer
office, she directed all the hubbub with staggering wisdom
and gut-wrenching humor. She not only performed expected
secretarial duties but also trained incoming clerks each year.
Our task was to think like a judge. We read briefs submitted
by two sides, analyzed the arguments, conducted our own independent research, and drafted an opinion that decided their
respective fates. The judge reviewed and revised the drafts,
treating with utmost care these court orders that would ultimately bear her signature. Joni looked out for us. She knew
the judge's expectations and helped us exceed them, often re-
working our written pieces so we'd appear brilliant in the
judge's eyes. Her writing and her grasp of legal principles suggested she'd be better placed behind an attorney's desk, but
that would mean leaving, in her words, "the best job in the
world."

Judge Crabb inspired that brand of loyalty. She had a job
for life, no need to fear reprisal for a bad attitude, but she
never wielded her power ungraciously. The bailiff, the pro-
bation officers, and the lawyers appearing before her all re-

ceived the same unerring, respectful treatment. And as law clerks, we got even better. There were three of us, all women. Susan, a Northwestern law grad, had a sunshiny disposition, a sincere spirit, and a wonderfully unspoiled existence as the daughter of U.W.'s chancellor. Jo, from U.W., had a husband, three school-age kids, and seasoned, perceptive opinions about most every issue placed before her. We were a solid team, supportive of one another and supported enthusiastically by the judge. She pumped us up with notes praising a job well-done and scheduled time each Wednesday to gather for lunch and listen to our personal stories. She magnified style to the nth degree, right down to the suits that lined her stately black robe.

If I'd had my druthers, I might have worked for Judge Crabb forever. But the clerkship term was one year—August to August. In September 1991, just one month into the job, I was already polishing my résumé and researching Madison's legal market. I learned that the three largest firms in Wisconsin are Milwaukee-based, and all have offices in Madison. I still preferred a large-firm environment, so I set my sights on the big three, having no basis upon which to distinguish them until I met Steve Crocker.

Steve walked into Judge Crabb's chambers as an unlikely candidate for the magistrate judge position. With his boyish face and tall, marathon runner's physique, he looked more like a candidate for Judge Crabb's next crop of clerks. But he had been inducted into that club years before and had returned to compete for a spot that would make him her peer. I met him on his way out and, after a few good minutes of conversation, deemed him pivotal to my job search. He was an attorney at Michael, Best & Friedrich, one of the big three, and served on the firm's recruitment committee. What's more, he told me the litigation department was in search of someone at my level. I fired off a résumé to the committee chair, and the firm granted me a half-day of interviews in early October.

The Michael, Best office, positioned in prime space overlooking the Square downtown, is within walking distance of the state and federal courts and across the street from the State Capitol. I drove over to remain fresh and unhurried and pulled inside the parking garage of the striking glass building at 1 South Pinckney Street. I rode the elevator to the top floor and stood in a reception area filled with dark wood and leather seating. A few feet in front of me I could see a glass-enclosed conference room and a spectacular view of the city.

"Hi, my name is Kim Cash. I'm here for an interview."

The receptionist handed over a schedule that lay in front of her. "Someone will be right with you. Feel free to have a seat while you wait."

Clutching a leather binder with extra copies of my résumé, transcript, and writing sample, I sat and studied the people walking to and fro, their interactions, and their conversation. According to my schedule, I would be meeting with several attorneys individually, then going to lunch with two more. I was happy to see Steve Crocker's name on the list, and began pondering what I'd say to him, when my first interviewer approached. He gave me a tour of the office space, then showed me to his office, where the interview began. A person not on the list joined us as well, and we talked well over our 30-minute allotted time. Steve conducted the second interview, which flowed seamlessly as anticipated. But when he escorted me to the next office, I was taken aback.

"Kim, this is Ruth Heitz. Ruth, Kim Cash."

A black woman stood up from behind her desk and shook my hand. I was shocked and relieved at once, wondering how I could have missed this tidbit in my research. Steve handed me his card, told me to call if I had any more questions, and closed the door behind him.

Ruth might as well have hugged me and said, "Sista girl, go on and have a seat and get comfortable," because that's exactly what I did. Instinctively, I knew I could get real in the interview and ask questions I could ask of no one else.

She had been at Michael, Best only a few months, and, yes, she really liked the people. Yes, she was the only black person in the firm—that's Madison, Milwaukee, *and* Chicago—but she could be herself and felt respected for it. And yes, the firm wanted more diversity but had a hard time attracting minority law students to interview, since most wanted to leave Wisconsin upon graduation. It sounded plausible.

I knew three things when I left home that morning. Michael, Best was a big firm. I wanted to work for a big firm. And Steve Crocker was a nice guy. By the end of the day, a bevy of reasons were shoring up my desire to work there. Ruth was one, certainly, but others impressed me as well. I met strong women, pregnant women intent on having it all, and men who thought the world of their families. I saw collegiality, an absence of hierarchy, and open doors. My gut said Michael, Best was the place for me, and my mind responded with hopeful anticipation. Just months earlier, my big-firm prospects were bleak. Well, actually, nonexistent. And here a door had opened before me. I was peering in, feet at the threshold, waiting for an invitation to enter. It could have slammed any minute, but I waited excitedly nonetheless. For two weeks. Then I got nervous. When two more weeks passed silently, I started mentally backing away. Then I got a call.

Steve Crocker left Michael, Best in January 1992 and joined us at the courthouse as a young and totally happy magistrate judge. On September 1, 1992, I crossed Michael, Best's threshold and walked into my own office with a beautiful lake view.

It was happening again. God's blessings, God's mercy I hadn't prayed for the job, hadn't even asked for it. He just made it His business to know. Despite tending to twentieth-century catastrophes and answering petitions of the faithful, He tuned in to Kim Cash in Madison, Wisconsin. He "heard" my desire and handed it to me, as most fathers with the power to grant their child's wishes would.

But I wasn't grateful, not really. I celebrated when I got

the offer, but Discontent came knocking and stole my joy. It was bigger than joy, bogging me down so I couldn't fully appreciate any positives that came my way. Having a job making more money than I needed wasn't enough. Building a new home within nine months of moving to Madison wasn't enough. Enough wouldn't be enough until I got on the first thing smokin' out of Madison with a banner promising, "Diverse City, U.S.A., or bust." So, no, I wasn't grateful. I didn't thank or praise God for gainful employment or a new roof over my head. I did summon Him, though, to speak to what I regarded as more pressing issues.

I had to know why I had been robbed of a life. I figured God was the architect of all I endured, but without the blueprint, I couldn't see where my "suffering" fit in. I didn't know if I was being punished or whether I was a pawn in someone else's flogging. I called His name, aloud some days, and demanded answers.

"God, tell me why I'm here. How long do I have to endure this? Why have you done this to me!?"

He existed again, and more often, if only for me to blame and berate. With each mental tantrum, I drew Him into my universe, recognizing He belonged there, desiring Him only for a limited purpose. He became significant in the evenings especially, when family members and friends reached out and touched. The opening dialogue differed only slightly, if at all.

"How's Bill?" a cousin or friend would ask.

"Oh, he's doing well."

"How's your job?"

"It's going well, too, busy as usual."

"So when are you moving back to D.C.? I know you can't wait to get out of there."

Never "Are you moving back one day?" or "Do you think you'll stay in Madison?" Just "When?"

"Who knows?" I'd say, and rush them to another subject, secretly lagging behind to mend their small talk's destruction. Presumably, my loved ones didn't know they had lobbed kindling into a smoldering fire. If left unchecked, it would breed and erupt weeks later. In the middle of some tame debate, I would blow up at Bill, sniping about how nobody could see us staying in Madison, so how in the world could he. I had to step inside myself, then and there, and warn my psyche, "This is chitchat, not ammunition. Let it go, and move on." Then, for my psyche's and my sake, I'd whisper, "God, you've got to get me out of here."

Our plane descended on darkness and an array of twinkling lights in the distance. I bubbled over with enthusiasm. The flight attendant directed us to remain seated, seat belts buckled, until the aircraft came to a complete stop. Since I was seated at the front of coach, right in her line of vision, I unbuckled it slyly, careful not to let the metal announce my defiance. With my torso as erect as possible, I stretched my right arm down and grabbed the handles on my carry-on luggage. The second the bell declared our official arrival, I took to the aisle. Then I looked back at Bill with irritation when his failure to break the rules slowed me up.

We got off the plane, walked inside Washington National Airport, and saw nothing but black. Black people representing various airlines. Black people working in airport gift shops and restaurants. Black people offering to help us with our luggage and scurrying about in taxi cabs. Black people milling about. I turned to Bill.

"Is *this* what I took for granted all my life?"

We hopped a shuttle bus to the car rental location. I got behind the wheel, and at that moment I sighed. I was home again. I had the power to drive to Tysons Corner and do some serious shopping if I chose, or head up the Baltimore-Washington Parkway to the Harbor for fresh seafood. I had options, wonderful options. I could swing through a museum and look at African art, peruse old R&B CDs at Roadhouse

Records, or just sit in a park and stare at a United Nations collective of people. I had no time for any of it. All that mattered was that I could.

I started the engine, but before I put the car in gear, I set the radio stations of my choice, all five of them. I had 48 hours to get caught up on the music scene. Black Entertainment Television played the hit videos, and it was better than nothing, but it was no match to radio. Slow jams from the 1970s and 1980s poured out of the radio. Club mixes of rap and go-go had a home on the radio. Donnie Simpson was on the radio.

For all of my radio-listening life, I awoke to that voice. It didn't use brash intonations or blurt out gimmicky one-liners. It just immersed itself in honey and sashayed all over the airwaves, dipping in and out of current events and sweetening the early-morning grind. Donnie had the "Chocolate City" wrapped around his finger, regaling us with personal stories about his wife and two children and weaving his infectious laugh through our hearts. I loved Donnie and so much as told him so in a letter sent care of WKYS. I wanted badly for him to respond. For days I got off the school bus thinking about the mailbox, halfway running to the mailbox. I was 14, young enough still to claim naïveté and enjoy it. One day I turned the lock with bated breath and saw it, turned sideways in our narrow box. A black-and-white picture of Donnie with his handwriting scrawled along the side.

"*To Kim, You're a wonderful young lady with big dreams. That's great. Keep dreaming and then make those dreams come true. Good luck and God bless you! Donnie Simpson.*" It hung on my bedroom mirror for an eternity, then graduated to my box of important notes and mementos, where it sits today.

As I grew older, Donnie's fame spread further. More and more of his personal stories featured personalities in the music and sports industries. It got so I looked forward to traffic jams on Monday mornings so I wouldn't miss the 411 on Donnie's weekends. We knew all about the opening of

Jimmy Jam and Terry Lewis's new Flyte Tyme studios in Minneapolis; the goings-on backstage at awards shows; and conversations on the putting green between him and Michael Jordan. He allowed us a peek inside popular places and lives and somehow pulled off an aura that he, too, was but a mere gawker.

That was the radio Donnie. He added BET's *Video Soul* to his schedule sometime in the mid-1980s, but I couldn't *feel* him on television like I could on the radio. The dynamics were too different. He was confined to scripted video introductions and occasional star interviews that concentrated on *them*. Evenings with *Video Soul* were fine when coupled with my Donnie-in-the-morning fix. But when I moved and lost the mornings, I lost a spot at Donnie's table, and *Video Soul* had no place for me to pull up a chair. I watched his hazel eyes anyway, grateful for the consolation prize, but missed the meals terribly.

I had been home numerous times since relocating to Madison, with and without Bill. Sometimes I made the trip just because. Just to get away. And Bill knew it, even encouraged it. D.C. revived my spirit, and he wanted more than anything for me to come back to life. He knew firsthand the effect Madison was having on me and on our relationship. My unhappiness was infecting our lives, and, though I was planning a big-deal wedding, it wasn't a foregone conclusion that one would take place. He was feeling extreme pressure to appease me, and he was all for a trip home if it meant temporary peace.

It was late October, one of those fall evenings when nature delivers a temperate breeze, and you close your eyes and murmur, "Ummm," to acknowledge receipt. I expected no less from D.C. It made the package for Homecoming 1992 that much more attractive. Maryland's Black Alumni Association planned festivities separate and apart from the official Homecoming agenda. It varied little from year to year. On Friday night, we would kick off the weekend with a happy hour at

Jasper's that would last into the night. Midday Saturday, we would tailgate before, during, and after the Homecoming game none of us would see. While mainstream folk cheered the Terrapins inside Byrd Stadium, we would listen to music, mingle, and grill hot dogs on LaPlata Beach, a field of splotchy grass across from LaPlata Hall and a stone's throw away from the stadium. Saturday night, those who hadn't tired of them would attend the step show, and most everybody would show up at the Homecoming party later that night.

Bill and I arrived in time for the happy hour. We planned it that way, left work early to make it happen. We pulled into the parking lot at about 7:30 P.M., and Jasper's was already brimming over. The line stretched down the sidewalk and out into the street. A security guard sat on a stool, arms crossed, attitude for days. When folks exited, he'd hold up two or three fingers to designate the number of people he would allow in next. If four came out and only two fingers went up, the crowd roared. "We're already beyond code," he'd bark, and end the matter.

On an average day, Jasper's management maintained its sanity. It was just another restaurant and bar in Greenbelt, Maryland, catering to the largely black crowd that lived nearby. But its close proximity to College Park made it fair game. Over the years, Maryland students and alumni targeted it for informal gatherings, and it had since graduated to embedded ink on a printed schedule every Homecoming season.

The reunion started in line, people yelling over top other people's heads, "What's up, fellas!" and "Hey, girl!" Faces sparked loads of memories. If the name had faded, I could always place the person vividly in a dorm, a class, the Union, wherever our worlds collided. And I remembered the vibes. If we didn't speak then, for whatever petty, long-forgotten reason, I maintained the status quo. One person I went out of my way to talk to, though, was Nicole.

I called her exactly one year after I clawed my way to the top spot in Eric's life. I was overcome with remorse, not due to a conversion on my part but because of the person I came to know her to be. If Nicole had been an evil person, even a normal person, I could have justified my actions. But she was too likable. No one I knew had a problem with Nicole. Much to the contrary, my often-critical friends were unanimous in their overwhelmingly positive regard for her.

I bit the bullet during the summer before my junior year while we were both staying on campus. I asked if I could come over and talk, and, incredibly, she said yes. I walked into her suite under a cloud of shame and apologized for my heartless performances. I waited for warranted soliloquies on what I had put her through, but without a single preface, she offered forgiveness. I had ruined any chance of our ever becoming friends, but we became openly cordial after that night, to the surprise of many who witnessed my treatment of her. The Caribbean crew was a different story, though. No matter how many years had passed, nothing moved me to speak to any of them. And despite my having never laid eyes on Alice again, they still rose to the top of my head at the mere thought of her. In my mind, *she* owed *me* an apology.

Inside, Bill and I stopped every few feet to hug and talk, in that order. Hugs were the greeting of choice at these gatherings. When people came face-to-face with an old acquaintance, even if they had never been real close, arms flung open and voices rose to a singsongy pitch.

"Heyyyy. I haven't seen you in so-o-o-o-o long. How are you-u-u-u-u?"

We found our flocks of close friends, hugged some more, and planted ourselves in the tight space they had groomed. The conversation, of course, turned to life in Madison, and it's only natural. Unlike Atlanta, Houston, Chicago, and the like, our circles had no familiarity with Madison. They'd never been there and never knew anybody who had been there. Bill and I had weathered a new frontier and were looked on as purveyors of knowledge about this foreign land.

"So, what's it like?" one asked sincerely.

"Oh, you know, it's your ordinary college town. It's really pretty. Surrounded by four lakes."

Another proceeded curiously. "But what is it really like? You know, for black people. . . . Are there *any* blacks out there?"

Bill and I exchanged looks that revealed what our friends suspected. Sensing they had struck a nerve, the crowd showered optimism.

"Well, you'll probably be back here in no time. Before you know it, Madison will be a distant memory."

I looked at Bill, and he understood my eyes to say, "Yeah, it better be."

When the crowd thinned, we left Jasper's and drove three miles down Greenbelt Road to Glenn Dale. Daddy and Joyce had moved from Kettering to nearby Glenn Dale the year before we left town. They were expecting us, though they didn't know what time. We rang the doorbell, and my brother Chris, after peeping out at us, giggled his trademark "Sorry, we don't want any." Seconds later he opened up, and my brothers Earl Jr. and Darian, Chris's co-conspirators, were right behind him. With every trip home the three of them stood several inches taller. Earl, 14, and Darian, 12, had surpassed me in height many visits ago. Chris, the youngest at 9, was well on his way.

We exchanged hugs and "hellos," and my brothers addressed immediately the first order of business. Before we could step beyond the foyer, Darian and Earl challenged Bill and Chris to a game on the backyard court.

"Are my runnin' shoes still upstairs, 'cause I didn't bring any with me."

"You know they're up there. We got you tomorrow, and don't try to get out of it," Darian warned.

"Oh, please. You and Earl can't check me and Chris. Matter of fact, we'll spot you a couple points so it'll hurt a little more when we take you to the hoop. . . . Nah, y'all don't need any points. You think you got skills."

Daddy was stretched out on the family room floor, remote control glued to his hand, switching every other second between two basketball games. Joyce was rustling up a late-night meal of fried pork chops and gravy, mashed potatoes, and green beans. She had a knack for cooking well all the foods we avoided at home—fried, buttery, fat-filled kinds of foods. Her most popular no-no's were sumptuous homemade rolls, known far and family wide. At Memorial Day gatherings, chivalry died the second the pan came out of the oven. The men trumped "Ladies first" with "First come, first served," and a couple used their weight to edge others of us to the back. Some, like me, took to lounging around the kitchen to get first dibs. When the batches slid out, we breathed a word to no one. Bill and I couldn't resist Joyce's melt-in-your-mouth meals. We just extended our workouts the following week.

"So, what's the score?"

Bill plopped on the couch, fixed his gaze longingly on the television set, and asked who was "comin' off." Daddy provided verbal replays of power rebounds and slam dunks, more than happy to oblige Bill's need to know. Their love of sports—statistics in particular—approached the fanatical. I could hang with them as long as the subject was headline news—starting quarterbacks, the nimblest wide receivers, Michael Jordan. But when they got passionate about 10th-round draft picks and third-string safeties, I took to the sidelines and watched with pleasure their familial camaraderie.

It took little time for Bill to worm his way into the hearts of my family. To my mother, he epitomized the son she'd never had. To Daddy and Joyce, he was son number four, one who didn't need permission to come over, nor a waiter once he got there. And to my brothers, he was 15 years younger, their peer, with stamina enough to run up and down the court all day and play computer games all night.

Dull moments didn't reside at Daddy's during our visits. Nor rested bodies. We were known to go well past midnight playing music and cutthroat games of bid whist, eating chips and dip, and talking about some of everything. This particular evening had similar leanings. It was already after 11:00 when we sat down with our plates, not at the table but on the sofa and chairs in the family room. Daddy, controller of all things electronic, had music drifting out of stereo speakers and the volume turned down on the television, except when he detected a worthy play. Family gossip was being traded like hot baseball cards. Laughter rising to fever pitches. I was feeling no pain, high off the luxury of being home and happy, when Discontent found me again, 800 miles away. It knocked that loud, insistent "I ain't goin' nowhere till you open up" knock. I stood my ground and kept laughing. It yelled under the door. *"Don't even get off into it. You're only here for two days, and then it's back to Madison."*

As long as competing voices surrounded me, jovial, loving voices, I was able to hold Discontent at bay. But then I retired for the night and lay staring at a dark, unadorned ceiling. Bill was downstairs on a pull-out bed, and I was alone with my thoughts. Alone with Discontent. It whispered in my ear, and I embraced it, cuddled up to it.

I had no cause to be happy anyway. I belonged in D.C., not living out of a suitcase on a two-bit weekend trip, but living. Madison would never be home, just a place I didn't plan to stay. So why was I there? Life was too short to succumb to such a tortured circumstance. I had been raised to be self-sufficient and independent. Why was I living according to someone else's plan? Did Bill really care about me or just himself?

I was half-asleep when Discontent slithered away with a satisfied grin. I had no idea I was being used.

Chapter 5

———◦◆◦———

De-Normalizing

THE DAY HAD NOT YET DISTINGUISHED ITSELF, AND I DIDN'T expect it would. It was August 27, 1989. Uncle Mann and Linda had just wed at Hemingway Memorial A.M.E. Church, and we were headed to the reception—Daddy, Joyce, and Chris up front; Earl, Darian, and me in the back. We arrived, and I opened the door on my right side as a car pulled in the space directly beside me. A beautiful black woman stepped out. She had a flawless brown face, darker than my brown, with big, round eyes. Her height and size mirrored mine; her hair hung above her shoulders, styled full of thick, relaxed curls. She was alone, and I smiled, guessing she belonged in Linda's extended family or circle of friends. Car doors slammed, and the group of us walked a few feet to the sidewalk. With the stranger and me side by side, heels clicking in step, Daddy announced casually, so casually, "Kim, this is your sister, Bonita."

We found the bond in each other's eyes and hugged tightly, immediately. My heart, blindsided though it was, opened wide and pulled Bonita into a place only a big sister could occupy. I had dreamed about her, longed for her on nights when my teenage heart ached and I needed to hear,

"It'll be all right; I've been there," echoed softly in the dark from across the room. I imagined the arguments a big sister and I would have over clothes, the phone, my wanting to hang with her and her friends. I had even given her a "K" name. "Kim and Karen" or "Kim and Kelly" made a dynamic duo, fending off all who dared mess with one or both of us. The premise, always, was ordinary siblings growing up together, living under the same roof, genetically linked to the same parents. This sidewalk scene belonged in a different script, one I never thought would play out in my lifetime.

If the Cash family had had such things as family jewels, they could have hidden the fact of Bonita's existence right alongside the diamonds and rubies. As it was, folk just carried it around with them, guarding it like the last bone to fall off our family skeleton. Daddy never mentioned her to me. His parents, five brothers, and two sisters never mentioned her. First and second cousins, great-aunts, if they knew, never slipped up. But my mother knew the deal, too, and schooled me on the family tree at an early age. She thought it my right to know that Bonita Emeral Wilkins was born three Decembers before me, prior to my own parents' marriage. My mother believed in open books, in full knowledge, and in protecting her daughter from the pain of secrets exposed abruptly and openly. Were it not for my mother, my jaw would have scraped the sidewalk, and my attention would have focused immediately on Daddy, questioning the "who" and, in particular, the "when." But from the moment of his pronouncement, my entire being focused on Bonita. My mother had prepared me to love her.

We clasped hands and walked united into the reception hall. One of my aunts hugged Bonita and whispered in my ear, "It's about time you two got together. I wanted to take you over there myself, but it wasn't my place." Grandma Cash hugged the two of us and dabbed her eyes repeatedly, then confessed under her breath to having invited Bonita after she stopped by Grandma's for a visit the week before. That's all I remember. If the bride and groom cut the cake, danced their first dance, or never showed up, I wouldn't know. I sat with my sister, who never knew I existed, and trudged through a painful history. For years, Bonita told me, she, her mother, and adoptive father lived in Kettering on Alistair, less than two blocks from Daddy and Joyce. I had close friends, twin girls, whose house I frequented during high school summers. She lived across the street.

Grief cast a haze over all things present as I traveled to what could have been. I felt sick, cheated, brokenhearted. My sister, age 25, had had her first kiss, her first serious disappointment, accumulated years of personal business, and I hadn't been privy to any of it. I knew nothing of her temperament, her talents, her food preferences. Had she grown up halfway around the world—New Jersey, even—I would have missed out on nothing more than a pen pal. But Bonita and I had lost real time, time we could have shaped and molded, made our own. We lost sister time, summer time, time when responsibilities were few and hanging time abundant. And we would never recoup it. Bonita had moved to New York the year before to attend the Fashion Institute of Technology. Time and silence had reduced us to pen pals.

"Bonita's mother didn't want me to be part of their lives. Her husband adopted Bonita when she was a little girl, and they just wanted to move on," Daddy explained over the phone.

Fine, I thought, twirling the cord around my index finger, my eyes rolled up in my head. That explains why you didn't send birthday cards or attend parent-teacher meetings, but I don't see what it has to do with Bonita and me sharing a sisterhood. I don't see what it has to do with keeping quiet about a sibling of mine whose house could be seen from your backyard.

"I just can't believe you never said anything," I sighed, almost to myself.

Daddy knew I wasn't satisfied, but he could offer no more justification than he had. Remorse permeated his pregnant pauses, and I might have heard it, had my bitterness not drowned it out. I was hurt, my mind regenerating the disappointments that dotted the landscape of our past. I wanted to sit down in them for a while, loiter in pain and self-pity. I could do it just fine from the distance of the telephone, away from the eyes that spawned mine.

Daddy's presence thawed my cold shoulders. I enjoyed him too much. His qualities, good and bad, form a magnetic blend. He's the life of the party, the one who sits back, arms folded, telling exaggerated stories about anyone in his line of vision. In his heyday (and he'd like to think still), he was flat-out cool. I've heard my mother recall the stunningly handsome Adonis who swept her off her feet at Bowie State College. The star athlete and quartet vocalist with dean's-list grades and a less-than-humble disposition. The kind of package that nabs women susceptible to big men on campus—a package that screams "Open Season" on unprotected hearts. I doubt he ever dreamed of counting a daughter among the bruised of his women. But I was the most vulnerable. By virtue of simply being, he had my undivided trust, my unconditional love. I depended on him, looked up to him, put my stock in him. If he let me down, I fell hard.

For a few minutes more, we fumbled with conversation surrounded by silence. I drew it to a close, sounding neither hostile nor forgiving, and hung up the phone. I didn't know if I could forgive. Forgiveness would mean casting away resentment. Forgiveness would mean I couldn't dredge up Daddy's role in the theft of our sisterhood whenever I felt like it. Forgiveness would mean allowing Daddy room to err, counting him human without a "super" in front. I wasn't ready to forgive.

Explaining my family situation became cumbersome. Once the question bore special meaning, I noticed how often people, virtual strangers, need to know whether one has siblings. To sudden acquaintances, I was an only child. To closer acquaintances, I was my mother's only child, with three brothers from my father's second marriage. Only to tight friends had I disclosed that I had a sister. I resented my inclination to hide Bonita. I had bought into the family habit, the unspoken pressure to keep Bonita bundled in secrecy. In 1992, I decided to unwrap her.

The decision to marry begets a million others, chief among them the size of the wedding and the number in the wedding party. Interested parties insisted that for a Cash–Tate wedding, a guest list of fewer than 200 would have been socially impossible. The check writer insisted that much over that would be financially impossible. Maintaining a reasonable number would prove a trying task, much like the selection of bridesmaids. I wanted a panoply of people culled from meaningful pieces of my life. I added, pruned, and sifted until I arrived at a manageable number—if nine females hailing from Maryland, Virginia, New York, New Jersey, Illinois, Texas, North Carolina, and Georgia can be considered manageable. Kim Hill, without question, was slated as my maid of honor. Though my contact with Lisa had devolved to a handful of times per year, our history wouldn't allow her to be anywhere but up front. I included a new friend, one who'd been dating Bill's cousin for years and with whom I had become close. And the rest would be family—cousins Yolanda, Sylvia, Sheree, and Danisha, Bill's sister-in-law, Tonja . . . and my sister, Bonita.

I wanted friends, old and new, to meet the newest addition to my family. I wanted family on all sides to recognize her branch, parallel to mine, on the Cash family tree. And mostly I wanted her to know our attachment was real and my love sincere. I realized she might decline the discomfort of watching her "father" celebrate the marriage of his only outwardly acknowledged daughter. But when I asked, she said she'd be honored.

The justice of the peace married my parents, so wedding planning, a universe unto itself, was new to both my mother and me. I embraced it. I have a personality trait that awakens when it senses an exciting undertaking is afoot. Bill calls it a "project mentality," an independent force that jumps in the driver's seat and carries me, and whoever is with me, on a whirlwind ride toward the goal, which is fine when all involved have agreed upon the goal. But more than once, Bill has had to stand in the street with a neon detour sign to turn it off-course. Like the time I got caught up looking for a new house. It started innocently. A "For Sale" sign went up in a yard I passed every day on my way to work, and I'd been intrigued by the home's design. I called the realty company, and an available person met me at the house and gave me a tour. I didn't like it and should have left it at that, but she began probing and set my mind working. Bill and I had built our house just one year before, but interest rates had fallen drastically, and we could get a good rate on a bigger home for not much more per month. I agreed to let the Realtor show me more houses. She mailed a pile of multiple listing sheets, I chose ones that looked interesting, and off we went one weekday evening. I found a gem, a beautiful soft contemporary with several upgrades, a pool (like we needed a pool in Wisconsin), and a list price that screamed, "Good deal." It had gone on the market that week, so I had to act fast.

I dashed home, pulled out a piece of paper, and dialed the number where Bill was staying in Accra, Ghana. He'd been there for three weeks, studying at the University of Ghana, and knew nothing of my antics. His roommate said he was at dinner, so I paced and fidgeted until I thought he'd be back. Speaking across continents, over a less-than-sparkling connection, I informed him of the marvelous opportunity that had fallen into our laps. I talked fast, as I often do in excitement, and ended by suggesting we make an offer. His better judgment said, "No," but he yielded and said, "Go ahead." Using his power of attorney, I signed both our names that evening on an offer to purchase, and the offer was accepted, but we included a contingency for the sale of our own house. If someone else came along without the same contingency, and we weren't willing to waive ours, we could get bumped. We did. A week later.

Bill was back by then and had actually seen the house and liked it but questioned whether we needed it anyway. The force kept moving. The woman of the house was sorry we got bumped and lent me their house plans so we could look into building a similar layout. I called our banker to get construction loan rates. Then, based on recommendations from co-workers, I called a builder and sat down with him and the plans, and we tweaked them a bit. Then I found a suitable lot, and Bill and I closed on it. We were ready to break ground, but we still had the hurdle of selling our house. We put it on the market and showed it for two weeks, and it was about that time that Bill slowed the force.

"Smooch [we call each other that], have we *really* thought about this thing? I know we've bought the lot and we have a big sign in our front yard, but have we *thought* about this thing? I mean, we built *this* house one year ago. No, we didn't get everything we wanted; we just wanted to get in our first house and build equity. But it *is* a four-bedroom house. A nice house. And anyway, you're always talking about trying to get out of Wisconsin. *Why are we moving to another house?*"

The question had ambled around in my subconscious, trying to reach the surface, but I had been batting it beneath the threshold. I was too far into my planning to concede quickly, but I knew he was right.

"You know I'm not tryin' to stay in Wisconsin. I'm ready to go right now. But it doesn't look like we're leaving anytime soon, so I need to do *something* to be happy while I'm here. This house is fine, but why not get in something we really like while the interest rates are low?"

He fired practical responses at my every justification until he brought to the surface my own reservations. I slept on it and returned to my right mind by morning. I canceled the showings scheduled for that day and asked our Realtor to get our house off the market and a "For Sale" sign on the plot of grass we were about to call home. Then I called the banker again, and we refinanced.

Project mentalities cover much ground on the way to the goal. Plans must be crafted, revised, and edited to perfection; notes must be kept of progress, contacts, and ideas; phone calls must be made, several sometimes just to get one answer; i's need dotting, t's need crossing. The overriding attribute is a desire to get it done, persevering in the face of "nos" and "maybes" and adhering totally to the concept "If it's anything worth doing, do it yourself." So when it came to my wedding, I divvied up planning duty with just one person. One who takes organization and responsibility even more seriously than I. One from whom I inherited my overarching need to regulate. My mother.

We attacked the infinite to-do list early, focusing first on the centerpiece of the event: the wedding gown. The subject had consumed me for months. The minute following my "yes" to Bill's proposal, I subscribed to *Modern Bride* and *Brides* and scanned hundreds of gowns and as many yards of tulle, Alençon lace, and silk shantung. My likes and dislikes came quickly to the fore. I definitely couldn't get with the *Gone with the Wind* look; I didn't want anything flaring out from the waist, no matter what the circumference. The Victorian look wasn't me; high collars and poofy shoulders reminded me of an age I was glad I missed.

My search, always, was for the classic, with a tinge of modern distinctiveness. I could never have described it to a seamstress, but I knew it when I saw it. It drew my eyes to the page and engendered a long, deliberate stare. I took in every inch of its substance. The dress fell softly below the shoulders, defining the back and neckline with delicate edges of sequins embroidered in silky satin. The bodice was form-fitting, sparkling with magnificence, and continued well below the waist, then dropped to a delicate flow of pure white satin. I hadn't seen anything like it. My eyes filled of the vision, and only then could my fingers turn the page, turning back often still. I placed a yellow sticker on the border for ease of reference and told my mother of my find.

She shared in my hunt by subscribing to the same magazines as I. On many an evening, I'd call with instructions like "Ma, turn to pages 112, 146, and 204 of the September issue of *Modern Bride*, and tell me what you think." Or we'd just flip through the magazines together and exchange editorial comments. We enjoyed the process, the creating of a bride, the sustenance of our mother-daughter bond. Bouncing thoughts and impressions off her kept us connected across the miles. My mother's opinions mattered. Frank, unfettered, and doused with love, they had influenced my steps, big and small. Whether I adopted her opinions or not, they held much value. And my wedding gown was no exception. Though I could have gone alone to survey them in person, I had no desire even to do a first cut without my mother's eyes in the place.

She flew to Madison for a long weekend, and we drove 60 miles to Margie's in Wauwatosa, the only Wisconsin store listed throughout the bridal magazines. It was the quintessential shopping event. Our sales associate settled us in a spacious dressing room with comfortable seating, bright lights, and floor-to-ceiling mirrors all around. I pulled three magazines out from under my arm and turned to the tabbed pages. She eyed them, scurried away, and returned with my three, a couple of others she deemed in line with my taste, headpieces, and gown-appropriate undergarments.

Like a personal handmaiden, she fussed with each—adjusting, tugging, pinning, and conforming—as I looked on from the square platform on which I stood. I saved my dream dress for last, let her get it just so, headpiece and all, then waited to see where it would take me. I turned to the back, the sides, got off the platform and walked around the room in the glittery heels she brought me, and saw Bill standing at the end of a long runway, watching me walk in slow motion toward him. I saw us dancing, him twirling me in full bloom, smiling as we rejoiced in matrimony. I saw full makeup, done-up hair, and long drop earrings to accent my bare shoulders. My mother saw it, too. We ordered it that day.

Bill and I wanted to get married in Maryland on Memorial Day weekend. And we wanted to get married in a church. A pretty church. We didn't have strong convictions about it, but when we asked ourselves, "Where?" we meant, "What church?" It was automatic. Pews, an altar, and a minister were wedding ingredients. People envision weddings in churches, much like funerals, which complicates matters for the engaged or the dead who have no church home.

We were thankful that we weren't reduced to scouting out an aesthetically pleasing church and twisting the arm of its pastor to marry a couple he'd never seen. We had Memorial Chapel, a picture of architectural splendor on the University of Maryland's campus. Alumni like us, devoid of church affiliation, could book a beautiful edifice for two hours, choose an affiliated minister off a preprinted list, and experience the wedding of their dreams. More than one year in advance, and just in time, I reserved May 29, 1993, and something close to our desired time. Days later, I received the list of ministers in the mail and perused their respective denominations. The Roman Catholic, I was sure, was white. Odds were good that the Methodist, Lutheran, and Presbyterian ministers were white. The Baptist minister could have been a black Baptist or a white Baptist. The only one on the list I could be sure was black was the one with "Black Ministries" under his name. That's the one I called.

By December 31, 1992, between my mother and me, we had contracted for the reception site, secured a photographer, videographer, calligrapher, florist, hairstylist, and makeup artist and enlisted the help of a wedding coordinator to order the vast wedding party on the day of the event. I had picked out bridesmaids' dresses and shoes, helped Bill pick out his and his groomsmen's tuxedos, and found a female disc jockey—I preferred my favorite songs over a group of musicians playing their rendition of my favorite songs. The sleeves on my wedding dress had been altered, long drop earrings, shoes, and pantyhose purchased, and professional photographs taken of the complete look in Maryland over the holidays.

But by January 31, 1993, Bill and I had switched gears.

Thinking about getting back in church is itself a big step for the wayward, so big that one can relax in the thought and stay an eternity. Bill and I talked about it for a good while in passing. We needed to invest in the stock market. We needed to call our grandmothers more. We needed to go to church. No immediacy attached to our proclamations, but they festered in our consciences and grew louder with time.

My burgeoning spirituality grew from a need to maintain my sanity. Built-up sadness had found me on the floor past midnight some nights, laid out in front of three-foot-tall speakers with music filling headphones clamped to my ears. I'd wait till Bill had gone upstairs to bed, then dim the lights and play slow, lonely songs as rivers of unhappiness flowed, releasing weeks of frustration, weeks of longing, weeks of fighting circumstance. My hands were tied. I couldn't leave Madison without leaving Bill, and I couldn't leave Bill without leaving part of myself. I was stuck. My life, clearly, had left my control—I lived and breathed in a place I hated—and the force of that reality was driving me crazy. I had to cope. I had to manufacture peace within. I surrendered to the One at the controls. Not the willing surrender that faith and trust bring, but a forced surrender motivated by zero alternatives. A limited and conditional surrender. I wasn't giving over my life to God. I gave Him my problem, in hopes He would fix it. And once I gave it, I walked with secret satisfaction. I complained still, but my complaints acquired a postscript. I ended "I can't stand this place" with "but God, I know you're working to get me out." Soon, I told myself, I could count Madison a mere blip on my screen of life, and I'd look back and find some contrived good in an otherwise lifeless experience.

Visiting God's home increased in priority. It seemed my end of my bargain, a tit-for-tat type of deal. I could ensure deliverance if I made appearances at Sunday service. It fit well with the perennial notion that it wouldn't kill us to get back to church. And *Catholic* church fit *real* well with both. Service was short, the attire come-as-you-are, the rituals common to both of us. St. Ann's was the natural choice. A relatively new church building with contemporary flair, it sat atop a hill a mere five minutes from our home and announced itself each day we drove to the university and downtown and home again at night. Sometime in summer of 1992, we stepped inside.

Gorgeous green plants lined the walls, and a cobblestone foyer led us to double wooden doors that opened into the sanctuary. The smells were of St. Margaret's. That burnt incense that clings to the air and reminds people they're on hallowed ground. The holy water was where I looked for it, just inside the sanctuary door, waiting on my fingertips to skim its bath. I dabbed it mechanically on my forehead, chest, and left and right shoulders, the four points of the cross, and looked around. There were no stained-glass windows like St. Margaret's. In fact, there were no windows at all. Bricks lined the interior walls, and light shone solely from five skylights above the pulpit.

The pews on the first floor were pretty well stacked, so we doubled back through the wooden doors and headed to balcony seating. Throngs of people kept filing in and seemed to know exactly the pew and row in which they wanted to sit. We stuck out like swollen thumbs. We were the only black people and might as well have been wearing signs that read: *"You've never seen us before. We haven't been to church in years. Sorry if we've taken the seat of one of you regular churchgoers."*

Being back in church had an old-shoe feel. Familiar. Comfortable. I knew the ordered service still like the back of my hand. The priest greeted us.

"The grace of our Lord Jesus Christ and the love of God and the fellowship of the Holy Spirit be with you all."

"And also with you."

I followed with my missal, half there, half back at St. Margaret's.

A layperson took to the lectern.

"A reading from the letter of Paul to the Philippians. '. . . So that at Jesus' name every knee must bend in the heavens, on the earth, and under the earth, and every tongue proclaim to the glory of God the Father: Jesus Christ is Lord!' The word of the Lord."

"Thanks be to God," we responded.

With each phase of the service, St. Margaret's came more vividly upon me until, inevitably, déjà vu called up a little girl whose soul had awakened in that place. She spoke to me.

"Don't you remember my connection to God?"

I did remember. I didn't feel the intensity, but I remembered. With open arms, I had come to God as a child and embraced His awesome power. For a moment in time, I was innocent and spirit-filled. Both had changed. I wondered what He thought of me, of what I'd become, of the things I'd done. I felt naked. I thought of my relationships. The sex we shared. My head fell, and "God forgive me" rang in my head.

The priest boomed, "This is the Lamb of God, who takes away the sins of the world. Happy are those who are called to his supper."

The congregation responded, "Lord, I am not worthy to receive you, but only say the word, and I shall be healed."

I had always said those words as if I, too, were about to take holy communion. I watched Bill go up, then retreated to my maudlin thoughts. When we left, my heart emerged heavy from the weight of reconnecting with my spiritual side but glad I had done something a level higher than where I'd been existing.

In the weeks following we returned to the balcony at St. Ann's. We developed a Sunday rhythm. Get up. Go to the 11:30 A.M. mass. Head home and eat homemade waffles in front of the Packers game. I had a spiritual life 45 minutes of the week. Well, 46. I began praying the Our Father in the morning as I readied for work. It was more like breezing through a spiritual moment than communing with God, but in my feeble way I was giving God His due.

My low-key spiritual side began flexing its muscle on occasion and cried out for a break from the "bump and grind" and "gangsta" lyrics that permeated video shows, my stereo system, and the tape player in my car. It needed conditions suitable for thriving, and, when I felt the urge, I obliged. Certain music already in my collection got more time. I played Patti LaBelle's song on her *Burnin'* album, "When You've Been Blessed (Feels Like Heaven)." "I Feel Like Going On," from the movie *The Five Heartbeats* got some time. Unlike Patti's, the song never mentioned heaven or a higher power, but it had full gospel flavor, enough anyway to stir a fledgling. When feeling most spiritual, I pulled out BeBe and CeCe Winans. I actually enjoyed these spiritual romps. I turned the music up, swayed, and sang out loud while my spirit drank up rejuvenation. It was a win-win situation.

But this low-key spirituality and I clashed when it got beside itself near the end of 1992, challenging much more than my choice of music. It got right down to the bone, gnawing at an issue near and dear to my existence. My living arrangement. It was no secret that Bill and I were living together. It made sense. We moved 800 miles together and planned to be married. Paying for two apartments never surfaced as an option.

Sharing a bed was nothing new for us, anyway. From one month into our relationship until the day Bill graduated, his roommates rarely saw him. We spent our evenings and nights together in Arlington. Bill had a key to my apartment, space in my closet, and shaving cream on my sink. I liked laying my head next to his at night. The commitment and dedication seemed stronger. I suspect my mother knew Bill was taking up residence there, but she never asked and I never told. She would not have approved. Her old-school moral code frowned upon "shackin'." Had she brought it to me, I would have huffed that we were adults capable of developing and living by our own code. I had little patience with uninvited interference.

Surprisingly, though, she condoned the Madison arrangement. An engagement combined with a move cross-country tipped the moral-code scales. She found comfort knowing Bill would be around to protect me in foreign territory. Still, she talked around the subject with friends and family and outright avoided it with my grandmother. I didn't care who knew. It was no big deal. We weren't forging new ground. And I wouldn't have cared if people had a problem with it. It would've meant simply that they needed to get a life.

I couldn't dismiss my own self that easily, though. Forty-six minutes of spiritual life said, "You can justify all you want, but you know you're wrong."

I beat it down. "Whatever. We're getting married in a few months."

It shot back, "Tomorrow's not promised."

I rolled my eyes but couldn't snap out a response. I didn't have one. I believed in a judgment day and heaven and hell. And I believed sinners were going to hell. I didn't think about it much, being young and invincible and all that, but I couldn't get around the fact that I was living in sin. And every day that passed until May 29, 1993, I'd be living in sin. The naked feeling returned. I imagined God looking down, right through the roof of the home we built together and into our bedroom. I wanted to hide.

I carried the turmoil alone for a while, hoping the guilt would pass. It didn't. So one day in the kitchen, I said tentatively, "Smooch . . . I think we should think about abstaining until our wedding day."

"What brought this on?"

"Well, I don't know. I've just been feeling like it's wrong. The whole sex-outside-of-marriage thing."

"Well, yeah. If you want to take it to that level, of course it's wrong. That's pretty basic. But since when have we cared about that? . . . I hear you, though. Maybe we should abstain. . . . Or better yet, we could just get married now, instead of waiting till May."

The idea seemed ludicrous. We'd been planning this wedding for a year. Was he suggesting we chuck it all?

Seeing the look on my face, he continued, "We don't have to cancel our May wedding, just get married early and tell only a few people."

It started to gel. I liked it. We talked about it more that night, and by the next day, I was off and running with my new project. It was nearing the end of January, and we needed a date. I suggested February 14, 1993, which fell on a Sunday. Bill had travel plans that weekend and was due back in town late evening. We went with the date and hoped a snowstorm wouldn't delay his plane.

I called Ruth. She had left Michael, Best and gone to an in-house position with a local utility company. I knew she had been appointed a court commissioner, with the power to marry. She agreed to officiate and volunteered her husband as a witness.

Then I called my mother, who was thrilled both with our decision and with being included. She purchased a plane ticket the next day.

Bill and I took our birth certificates down to the Dane County Clerk's Office and got a marriage license. I ordered a heart-shaped ice cream cake from Dairy Queen with "Happy Valentine's Day and Congratulations" in red lettering atop the icing. Bill selected the champagne. And I went looking for a dress to get married in. Again.

Time confined me to Madison stores. I wanted something special, not too ornate or overblown, and I began my search in Marshall Field's. I flipped through the racks of evening and special-occasion dresses and spotted an eggshell-white dress with a square neckline and muted gold beads hand-sewn on the front. It had long sleeves and rested just above the knee. I found my size and carried it to a dressing room one-quarter the size of our suite at Margie's and half as well lit. With no handmaiden in sight, I pulled it over my head myself, zipped up the back, and assessed the look. It was perfect.

Plans to get right with God had a startling effect. For the first time, I recognized Bill as my soul mate. He had been lover, best friend, boyfriend, and fiancé. Never soul mate. It was as if God was saving that special revelation, wanting first to see whether we cared about our souls. He had watched our wedding plans unfold without mention of Him and witnessed our superficial desire for a church wedding. God waited, and when finally we demonstrated some regard for Him, He unlocked the secret to Bill and Kim. I saw it just as easily as God taking a paintbrush to an easel before me. Bill was never *my* choice, but God's, handpicked just for me. Our meeting, our dating, our moving to Wisconsin, had been preordained—the "why" yet to be seen. I could feel the love blossoming, a deep connection forging, as we climbed out of our state of disobedience. Knowing God blessed our union, that our union had a purpose, blew my mind. A spiritual relationship. I had never known such a thing. It made sense of my holding on to Bill when all else said, "You're not happy here. Leave." I had attributed the pull to the beating of a lovesick heart, when it was my soul, coiled with his, calling the shots.

Past 10:00 P.M. on February 14, Bill and I stood in front of our fireplace and pledged for better or for worse. Candles blazed. Roses scented the air. Five people witnessed, instead of 200. No photographer snapped our every move. No limousine waited to whisk us away. And no honeymoon in the isles would see us that week. But God was in the front row, in our home at our invitation. And as we said, "I do," a weight lifted from my soul, and I embraced Him once again, in all His glory. My orbit traveled still some distance from the light, but I had rotated a little bit toward it.

Chapter 6

——⊰·◈·⊱——

R&B Love Affair

I WAS SEDUCED BY R&B MUSIC AT AN EARLY AGE. IT WAS intoxicating, chock-full of luscious harmonies and pulsating rhythms. I drenched myself daily: in the bedroom, in the car, in the shower, even in my sleep. The pull was magnetic, the gratification immediate. It calmed me in emotional storms, uplifted me in celebration, soared with me on sentimental journeys. And though the music itself arrested me, my interests expanded beyond passive listening. I paid attention to the placement of cymbals and guitar strings and the extraordinary talent of background singers.

I knew the hot and not-so-hot writers and producers associated with R&B artists as well as which artists wrote and produced their own material. I noted the record companies to which R&B artists were signed, the songs that went gold and platinum, and the Grammys and American Music Awards that were handed out year to year. I was immersed in it all. But as much as I might have fancied myself an industry aficionado, I was a complete outsider. Until 1994.

It began one January evening when cooking and cleaning seemed to be my sole excitement. A melody barely audible caught my ear, and I stopped, walked to the television set, and turned up *Video Soul*. Six guys I couldn't readily identify had a 1970s-style thing going on—playing real instruments, singing about real love—reminiscent of the Commodores or Earth, Wind & Fire. No women appeared in the video. Just the band working out in a warehouse jam session.

The song pinned me in place until the video ended and sent me to my local Best Buy store the very next day. I bought Mint Condition's CD, and the tape for my car, and played "U Send Me Swingin'" before work, on the way to work, and on the way home from work. At night, I cranked it up in my headphones to magnify the nuances. The mix was so full, so lush, I'd get lost in a different section on each replay. Sometimes I'd flow with the keyboard arrangement and drift on the melody. Sometimes I'd get caught up in the snare and mumble in amazement, "This drummer is a *bad* boy." Other times, I'd focus on the romantic imagery of the lyrics or the tight three- and four-part harmonies. But mostly I concentrated on the lead singer, Stokley (who happens to also be the drummer and the background harmony).

My favorite male crooners have voices of mighty distinction. No matter how strong the effort at imitation, no one can invade the territories of Luther Vandross, Ronnie Isley, and the late Philippe Wynn. They have a golden signature, recognizable from the opening note of even an unfamiliar song. When I hear them, whether I planned to or not, I listen. I have to, understanding that talent so rare deserves an undivided ear. I inducted Stokley into my "club" of exceptional vocalists soon after I bought Mint's album.

His voice is thick and rich like syrup, total substance. When Stokley sings, the air fills with his presence, to the point of domination, and the ear stirs by force of beautiful, unparalleled sound. He's crazy versatile, cruising a smooth tenor naturally but detouring effortlessly to feathery falsettos and soulful bottoms. At a serenade's height, his specialty, his voice brims with unbridled emotion, leaping across octaves as if one step ahead of a fiery blaze.

Stokley's talent so blew me away I had to tell him. I sat in front of my computer on January 24 and typed my second piece of fan mail. In a short note, I expressed appreciation for Mint's album and sent kudos to band member Keri Lewis for writing "Swingin'." But I went beyond that. As I stared at the screen, words to a poem clicked in place, and, when complete, it described the way Stokley's voice lifted me up out of my chair, my car seat, my couch, wherever I happened to be, and sent me soaring to musical highs. It spoke of the power of music, the power of talent, and the willingness of this particular passenger to take the ride.

I printed my note and poem on colored paper, sealed them in a matching colored envelope, and paused. I couldn't have my fan mail going the traditional fan-mail route, relegated to a heap of "P.O. Box" messages Stokley might never see, let alone open. I dialed Minneapolis information and got the number for Flyte Tyme Productions, the studio home to hit-makers Jimmy Jam and Terry Lewis. Mint Condition, also out of the twin cities, was signed to their record label, Perspective.

"Flyte Tyme."

"Hi. I have some mail that I want to send to Stokley, and I know there's a fan club address in their CD insert, but I just wondered if you could give me a better address to send it to."

I knew I had a lot of nerve, and I waited for him to say, "All I can tell you is to send your correspondence to 'Mint Condition Fan Club, P.O. Box. . . .'" But he was kinder than that.

"Well, I can't give you Stokley's address, but I can give you his manager's number. Wait a minute."

I could hear the computer clicking.

"Okay. Here's Popeye's number."

He read it to me; I thanked him generously and hung up the phone. Immediately I dialed Popeye's number, hoping I wouldn't get the brush-off and wondering why the name sounded so familiar.

Someone answered, "We care for music."

"Hi, is Popeye there?"

"This is Popeye."

I stopped breathing for two seconds. I didn't think I'd reach him and certainly didn't expect him to answer. I relayed my story of wanting to send mail to Stokley and not wanting to go the fan-club route. He asked my age, curious whether he had a teenager with a teenage crush on his hands. When I told him I was 27 with a passion for music and mad appreciation for his band, he seemed satisfied, and the conversation branched to other areas.

Popeye asked what I did for a living and what interests I had in music. I shared my suppressed desire to be in the business—singing, songwriting, whatever—and confessed I had no experience in any of it. He launched into a tutorial of the music business, lyric writing, and demo production. He had producers who could put music to lyrics, a studio in which to record songs, and contacts at record labels. My mind raced. I asked if he'd be willing to critique my lyrics (as yet unwritten) and he agreed, but I needed more. I secured a date to meet in February, determined not to let the opportunity lag, then returned to my reason for calling.

More than one hour had passed, and we had established a friendly repartee. Popeye gave me *his* P.O. Box address with the assurance he would pass my letter on personally. The offer was far better than the fan-club option, but I had a bias against P.O. Box addresses. I asked whether he had a street address, and after mumbling something about hoping he could trust me, he gave me the connection I sought. I thanked him and said I would call in a couple of weeks to confirm our meeting.

Amazing restraint kept me from calling Bill the instant I hung up. I wanted to regurgitate my news while still in the moment, but my conversation with Popeye had lasted into the evening, everyone had left the office, and I wanted to get home. I pulled into the garage hoping Bill wasn't on the phone or, worse, taking an early-evening nap. I opened the door and found him in perfect position, in the kitchen and unoccupied. I replayed the evening's events, down to the lines of the poem I had written, and ended with my plans to write lyrics and have them critiqued by Popeye.

I don't know what I expected him to say. With stern disapproval, he could have asked whether I had plans to leave my paying day job and dedicate my waking hours to the music biz. Or he could have challenged my excitement by asking simply, "Have you thought about this for one minute?" But Bill knew well my love of music and knew better than to shoot me down before I took to the air. He showed genuine enthusiasm, supported the growth of my wings, and waited, as I, to see where they would take me.

Alexander O'Neal's *Hearsay* album had power. When I played it, body parts moved without the slightest bit of direction from me. Hands clapped, hips swayed, head bobbed from left to right. All, most times, while I drove my car and was confined by the seat belt.

Kim and I must have played *Hearsay* dozens of times during road trips senior year at Maryland. It was one of those rare albums we didn't have to fast-forward through to get to two, maybe three, decent offerings. Song after song packed a jammin', feel-good, funk-filled groove that took us down the highway for hours without cares of time, fatigue, or boredom. *Hearsay* is, literally, a party. When the album begins, before the music rolls, O'Neal greets his guests as they arrive— Jimmy Jam, Terry Lewis, Jerome, Jellybean, and "my main man Popeye." And between songs, party dialogue takes place. In the intro to the song "Fake," glasses clang loudly, causing a woman to spill wine on a man's "40-dollar shirt." The man complains, and one of the fellas asks, "You all right, Pop?" Popeye sighs, "Naw, man, messed my shirt up."

I had been anxious to figure out why "Popeye" had rung a bell from the time it rolled off the Flyte Tyme receptionist's lips. That same night, I dusted off tapes and CDs produced by Flyte Tyme—Janet Jackson's *Rhythm Nation*, the New Edition *Heartbreak* album, Cherrelle's *Affair*—and saw "James 'Popeye' Greer" listed under Flyte Tyme's staff as operations manager. I might have been satisfied that I had simply scanned the name several times before, but then I got to O'Neal's insert, saw James "Popeye" Greer listed as a "fake fella" and a "party guest," and played the *Hearsay* album. The mystery cleared immediately, and in its place came a stirring realization.

A new song had unearthed an old favorite, and a connection common to both . . . *my* new connection. In one evening, unexpectedly, a window of anticipation had opened, ushering in a fresh spring breeze in the dead of a Wisconsin winter. The possibilities, I concluded, were endless.

Beginning the day after I committed Popeye to reviewing my lyrics, I fixated on writing them. The endeavor totally consumed me. Melodies popped into my head all times of day and woke me up out of my sleep at night, and lyrics floated through my mind with the speed of lightning. My Dictaphone, which I had never mastered at work, stayed in arm's reach so I could record ideas the second they surfaced. In time I had six songs, five of them slow to mid-tempo, all of them about some dynamic of love. They were my babies. Each had its own unique melody, its own emotional feel. I knew precisely the way they should sound, but on paper, they were nothing more than words. I realized I would have to breathe life into them for Popeye. And the only way I knew to do that was to record myself singing the lyrics. Anxiety rushed through my veins and paralyzed me in fear.

I sang early and often in my youth. Alone. Away from listeners. Teena Marie, Angela Winbush, and Patti LaBelle instructed me. Their vast ranges challenged and inspired. On my old turntable I'd place the needle on the song I wanted to hear and begin my lesson. I would strive to hit every inflection, every ad-lib, every high note. If I got a word wrong or cut off a riff prematurely, I'd lift the needle and put it back to the beginning until I got it right. But as much as I loved to sing, I never sang in school choirs or talent shows. My passion was too great to risk rejection. I contented myself with living a private dream, giving private concerts in the sanctity of my teenage bedroom.

Time didn't change the rules. Outside of the WKYS singing contest, I never sought or received formal feedback on my voice. I never took seriously this child's dream of stages and microphones. And yet, without warning or sanction from the rule-making majority, a part of me had gone and acknowledged the truth of the fantasy and put a foot toward pursuit of it. In the process, it was giving Popeye the power to ruin a lifelong vision. From one conversation, I knew he would be honest, and it scared me. If he thought I was wasting my time, he would say, "You might want to rethink this."

With great trepidation, I succumbed to my inner whims and decided to record my voice on amateur equipment with no musical accompaniment. I bought a microphone, plugged it into my tape deck, and pushed the RECORD button. My voice shook with nervousness, causing me to erase repeatedly and record over until I got a grip. Somehow all six songs made their way onto the tape, and I became halfway excited about getting some feedback.

I called Popeye a few days before our scheduled meeting and had a bit of the wind taken out of my sails. Mint Condition was set to replace Tony Toni Toné as Janet Jackson's opening act on her *Janet* tour, and Popeye would be on tour with them for a few weeks. He couldn't reschedule, because he didn't know the date of his return, but he told me to call back in March.

I didn't sulk long over the interruption in plans. I had

tickets to see Janet in Milwaukee on February 7 and was thrilled that I would see Mint as well. Bill and I had good seats at the Bradley Center, courtesy of the firm's advance tickets, and arrived before the show started. I watched closely as a variety of men moved equipment and walked the stage, making final checks. One of them had to be Popeye, I thought, and imagined which face would likely go with the voice.

My mind was in another place during most of the show, wishing I could find an access door, get security to find Popeye, and get Popeye to let us hang backstage. And I would have tried, too, but I knew Bill would call me crazy and demand I chill, so I kept my desires to myself. Curiosity increased when the show ended. I saw the secured corridors, roped off to separate the riffraff from the performers, and my eyes loitered, as if to catch a surprise glimpse of a Mint band member or a Janet dancer. I wondered where they were going afterward, whether they were staying in town. I felt an urge to be in the inner circle, behind the scenes, but I left like everyone else in the crowd, going down a designated stairway and into the public parking lot.

I phoned Popeye periodically in March to see if he had returned. I never left messages. Waiting for a return call takes one out of the driver's seat, and I like the driver's seat. He picked up the phone one day and said they would be leaving again in a couple of weeks.

"How's next week?" I asked.

On Friday, March 7, I drove 3½ hours to St. Paul, an easy, straight drive west on Highway 94, and pulled in front of Popeye's Victoria Street address at about noon. I knocked, and no one answered. I knocked several times more. No answer. I went to my car to make sure I had the right house. I did. Puzzled, I drove to a local mall and called. No answer. I got annoyed and started talking to myself.

"No, I didn't drive all this way for him to leave me hanging like this."

I waited and called again. No answer. Then I called Flyte

Tyme and asked if Popeye was there. A few seconds later, I heard, "Hello, this is Popeye."

"No, you didn't just leave me hanging!"

"Kim! Oh, I'm sorry. I got caught up here at the studio working on this song. Oh, I'm sorry. Tell you what. Can you meet me up here? It's not too far. I'll give you directions."

Could I meet him at Flyte Tyme?? Was he questioning whether I minded? The anger frittered away, and elation flooded in its place. I think I even said, "Thank you, God."

I pulled into the parking lot of an unlabeled, nondescript building, went to the second door as instructed, and rang the doorbell. A six-foot-tall gentleman in glasses, overalls, and a Spike Lee Joint jacket opened the door. I figured it was Popeye, and once I made sure, I harassed him for standing me up, failing to mention my gratitude for doing so.

I met the receptionist who had linked me to Popeye and glimpsed a long hallway lined with framed albums bearing Jimmy Jam and Terry Lewis's imprint. Janet hung prominently, New Edition, Herb Alpert, Patti LaBelle, Johnny Gill, Alexander O'Neal, and many others.

We walked through an eating area with award-covered walls, around a corner, and up a flight of stairs to a game room with more framed albums and a life-size cardboard statue of Janet. Popeye took my tape and popped it into a stereo system, took the lyric sheets, lay down on the floor in front of the stereo, and listened quietly. I sat behind him on a couch, embarrassed by the sound of my bare voice, wanting to jump out the window. The sixth song ended, and I braced myself for the worst.

Popeye stood up and said matter-of-factly that I had raw talent, that I should take lessons to learn to properly use my vocal instrument, and that my lyrics needed work—not enough hypnotic hooks. I could live with that.

His cell phone rang. It was Stokley calling from the parking lot, ready to lay the drum track on the song Popeye was working on. We walked down the stairs, and, with coat in hand, I thanked Popeye for meeting with me and critiquing my work. He asked if I wanted to stop inside the studio for a minute, and, with understated, restrained enthusiasm, I replied, "Sure."

We walked through the studio door and smack into Stokley. He was dressed comfortably in jeans and a T-shirt, a bit taller than he appeared on screen. He smiled and shook my hand after Popeye's introduction and went to the recording booth to play the drums. Popeye, a guy named Roger, and an engineer sat at the boards, and I sat in a seat behind them, marveling at the elaborate equipment and the process of creating a song. A new male group signed to the Warner Brothers label would record the vocals the following week. This studio session would tighten up the music. The portion previously recorded looped over and over, and Stokley played the drums over and over until the product pleased all concerned. I was engrossed totally, wanting to work the equipment myself like a pro, wishing my day job held such inherent fascination.

The studio door opened, and Terry Lewis walked in, nodded hello, and retrieved what he came for. He was without the trademark fedora and dark shades he wore in interviews, strictly at home in a sweat suit and tennis shoes. I pretended to barely notice.

I called Bill from the phone in the eating area to explain why I was still in Minneapolis. As I headed back to the studio, Stokley rounded the corner. I asked if he happened to read my letter. He said he hadn't seen it, which didn't mean he hadn't received it, just that he hadn't gone through his mail. I gave him the face-to-face version, down to the degree to which I was driving my husband crazy playing "Swingin'" 20 times per day. He was humble and casual; I was teetering between cloud nine and overload. I had awakened that morning excited about a feedback session with Popeye, and the day had delivered Flyte Tyme, Terry Lewis, and a conversation with The Voice. I wanted to hold him there, pick his brain about music and the industry, find out how he liked opening for Janet. But he was headed out, and I needed to leave as well. I said my goodbyes with little pleasure, got in my car after 8:00 P.M., and popped in the Mint tape. When I rolled into Madison around midnight, I had turned the day over in my head a million times.

Popeye spent his early years in Omaha, Nebraska, where he became acquainted with a very young Terry Lewis and Terry's younger brother, Jerome Benton. His family later moved to the Twin Cities, where Popeye sang with a band as a teenager and, in his early twenties, ran the spotlight for a local band called Flyte Tyme, led by Terry Lewis on bass. Flyte Tyme evolved into The Time, with Morris Day, Terry, Jerome, Jimmy Jam Harris, Jellybean Johnson, and others. While The Time fired up the charts and opened for Prince on tour, Popeye worked in the Minneapolis school system. But when Jimmy and Terry returned to open Flyte Tyme Studios in the mid-1980s, Popeye came on board as operations manager and stayed until he heard a local band playing live at the Riverview Supper Club, became their manager, and helped get them a deal with Jimmy and Terry's new label, Perspective Records.

Maybe it was our love of music. Maybe it was our love of Mint Condition's music. Popeye and I clicked. At 43, he could have played the role of father figure, but our interactions were more akin to siblings'—disagreeing freely and comfortably and giving each other unsolicited advice. We talked almost daily, often about his knowledge of the industry and his varied experiences. He enjoyed educating me. "All that glitters is not gold," he'd say, and explain that many full-glam artists strutting their stuff on *Video Soul* are broke or that the business in general is cutthroat. But he was too familiar with the love to discourage me from pursuing an entree into music. He merely suggested another point of entry.

"Why don't you get some books and learn about entertainment law?"

At once attractive and ludicrous, the idea danced slowly in my head. In law school I had dreamed the dreams of representing big names in entertainment, and even attended meetings of the Entertainment and Sports Law Society, but never seriously leaned that way. It seemed too pie-in-the-sky, and to be for real, my center needed to be Los Angeles or New York. I planned to stay in D.C. The thought of jump-starting an entertainment law practice out of Madison was about as backward as launching an all-night soul food diner there. But as Popeye continued, I listened.

Talent abounded still in the Twin Cities. Up-and-coming producers had studios in their homes and worked till all hours of the night creating what they hoped would be hits. Often they partnered with up-and-coming vocalists in need of the all-important demo tape. The team would put together a handful of songs that best showcased the singer's voice and the producer's music, then shop the tape to industry professionals. In the best of circumstances, both would get a break— the artist would sign a record deal, and the label would use the producers to work on the album. Popeye had a network of producer friends striving for that big break, friends who would likely need a lawyer to negotiate any number of contracts on their behalf.

At his prompting, I bought books that detailed the business and pored over them in the evenings and on weekends until mechanical royalties, compulsory licenses, and controlled compositions swam in my head. I also found myself in the Wisconsin State Law Library, asking for legal reference books on music law. I left carrying a weighty treatise with sample contracts between manager and artist, artist and record label, label and producer, and umpteen other variations. The book gave exhaustive explanations for each provision of each contract and emphasized particular points every competent lawyer needed to at least try to win for his or her client.

Within weeks, I had my first entertainment client. Popeye.

He received a production contract for a song he co-wrote and co-produced, the one he had been working on at Flyte Tyme during my visit. He trusted me to represent him, and I relished the opportunity to get hands-on experience. I negotiated against an L.A. lawyer who, presumably, had tons of experience and handled deals like this one in his sleep. I spoke with authority to disarm skepticism about this middle-America entertainment lawyer and proceeded point by point down my pages of prepared notes. Over a few days, we engaged in the obligatory back-and-forth as I held firm to positions my treatise insisted I take.

I thought, What if the book is outdated? What if a recent shift in wisdom just occurred regarding these very issues? Surely he's wondering why he's been forced to deal with an amateur.

Then I thought, Okay. These points are valid and ones I needed to raise, but every other attorney knows the record company never caves and has given up by now. Surely he's wondering why he's been forced to deal with an amateur.

My fledgling career in entertainment got a boost when the final contract incorporated concessions I was after. I gained an ounce of experience, a pound of confidence, and grander visions of the future just as another potential client came my way.

Producer friends of Popeye's had completed a demo for a female group and wanted to sign them to a management/production contract. Popeye drove two members of the production team to Madison on May 8, Mother's Day, so they could meet with me and decide whether to use my legal services. I had a new client before they left my house and returned to Minneapolis the following week to meet with them again.

My second trip rivaled the first. I checked into the Radisson in downtown St. Paul Friday afternoon and drove over to Popeye's. He had a quaint home with Mint memorabilia on the living room walls and an attic taken over by a recording studio. He had just finished the studio tour when

Stokley walked through the front door. He greeted me warmly with a handshake and small talk, and I looked on as they talked logistics of getting Mint's instruments to Ohio for a weekend concert. I still regarded Stokley with awe. Not romantic infatuations, but sheer amazement at his talents. Over my lifetime, many artists had captivated me, but none had ever been in my immediate presence. Had he been full of himself, the aura would have died straight away. But he came off like he was nothing special, cementing my admiration all the more.

I saw Stokley a second time that evening when Popeye stopped by the Riverview for the Sounds of Blackness's album-release party for *Africa to America—The Journey of the Drum*. For Popeye, the scene was typical, but typical for me was not bumping into faces I recognized from videos and album covers. Popeye introduced me as his lawyer to these faces, and I watched as they mixed and mingled. I wondered what it would be like to live in a music city and regard such sights with blasé indifference. *Real* indifference. Not the "I'm not fazed (but really I am)" demeanor I had going. But as I tripped inside over my surroundings, some tripped on me. They had never met a black female lawyer, they said, and wondered to my face whether I was for real.

"So you've passed the bar? Are you practicing? Really?"

The exchange repeated itself with regularity. And each time I gave assurances that I was legit, I could sense my invisible ink fading as the person saw me for the first time, right then. I was no longer just another female hanging out at the club on Friday night. I was an attorney, and whatever significance they attached to that seemed enough to separate me, however slightly, from the crowd. I was grateful for the edge.

I met with my new clients on Saturday in their home studio and also met the female group with whom they worked. The group had just gotten back their professional photos, which completed their demo package, and Popeye, I learned, would be going to Los Angeles in two weeks to shop the act. Privately I asked whether I could travel with him. I wanted an inside view of the process and a greater understanding of this business I was rapidly devoting myself to. He agreed to my tagging along.

On my way out of town on Sunday, I planned to spend a minute at Popeye's saying goodbye and hit the road, but my exit was delayed. He asked if I wanted to record my voice in the studio, and I couldn't resist. Since my first visit, I had been taking lessons. An acquaintance pointed me to a choir director at Mount Zion Baptist Church, and we began meeting on Saturday mornings. Jackie taught me that the voice is an instrument that needs to be warmed up, tuned, and properly cared for, much like the clarinet I played in junior high. I learned the breathing exercises that awaken the instrument and how to breathe during singing to achieve power and longevity. And I had been serious about my homework, banging out the scales on a keyboard I bought just for that purpose and singing vocal exercises in a book she provided.

Popeye had promised I could test my progress in the studio one day, but I hadn't expected his indulgence so soon. I had no high notions of fitness for the task, nor had I conquered my fear of singing before an audience. But the prospect of getting a real taste of the dream overwhelmed my inhibitions.

He cued up an old demo tape of a woman singing a beautiful ballad written by one of Mint's band members. I listened a few times and wrote down the words, then Popeye moved a lever on the boards that eliminated the lead vocals. I stepped inside the recording booth, put on the headphones, and practiced singing lead with the music and background vocals. I couldn't see Popeye, which was good, so I sang with all the feeling I mustered routinely in my car and shower.

I kept hearing through my headphones, "Breathe. You're not breathing."

"What do you mean? I can't sing without breathing. I have to be breathing, or else I would have passed out by now."

I got frustrated. I thought I was doing okay for my basic level of expertise, but he wasn't hearing what he thought he should. He recorded my effort and told me to listen to it at home and continue practicing.

I didn't wait until I got home. For most of the drive to Madison I played the tape and marveled at how different I sounded in that medium. I played it for Bill and, later, for my mother, and Daddy and Joyce. To untrained ears, I wasn't that bad. Better, actually, than they expected. Like Bill, my parents had no idea where I was going with this escapade, but neither did I. I was living in the moment, happily paired with opportunity, doing all I could to make the most of it.

I waited outside the office of the administrative partner at Michael, Best and walked in when he hung up the phone. I told him of my long-range plan to develop business in the entertainment area, about the connections I was acquiring in nearby Minnesota, and about this chance to travel to Los Angeles to make additional contacts. He wasn't convinced as to the ultimate success of my endeavor but supported my entrepreneurial spirit and authorized payment for plane fare, hotel accommodations, and expenses. On June 1, I flew from Madison to Minneapolis, connected with Popeye at the airport, and flew with him out to California.

Popeye had an appointment with Cheryl Dickerson, vice president of A&R at Epic Records, the afternoon our plane landed. We walked into her spacious office, and she and Popeye received each other like old friends. He pulled out the demo tape, photo, and biographical information and talked up the group like they were the next Supremes. Cheryl popped the tape in the stereo behind her desk and listened for less than one minute to the first song before fast-forwarding to the next. Her head bobbed a little, like she was trying to like it, but she had an expression that said something wasn't quite right.

Cheryl walked out of the office and returned with Faye Baxter, an associate of a big tour promoter. As far as I could understand, the promoter and Epic were working on a label deal, and Faye was looking for talent to kick off the label. Cheryl played the tape for Faye, and she, too, stared ahead with a slight bob of the head and a wrinkled brow. The two agreed the lead singer had a great voice, but the group needed an image, a better picture, and better music.

We left Epic, walked across a courtyard to Columbia Records, and met with a guy who had little interest in our reason for being there. He paraded around his office, talking excitedly about artists he had just signed and playing samples of their music. He asked about Mint Condition, said he'd love to sign Stokley, and, finally, gave an ear to the group we wanted signed. I don't know how he could have listened critically while talking constantly and shuffling papers, but he announced in a so-sad voice that it really wasn't the sound he was looking for, and, really, he had no need for a girl group right then.

The following day we walked into a huge reception area at MCA Records to meet with Louil Silas Jr. I had a special interest in that meeting. Years before, I had listened to Louil and Cassandra Mills, of Giant Records, at a music seminar at the Smithsonian Institution. He struck me as self-confident and knowledgeable, definitely on the upswing, someone to know in the industry. Popeye and I waited and watched a wall-long screen of MCA artists' videos until we got word Louil couldn't break free. Popeye left the package with the receptionist, then drove to Giant Records and left one for Cassandra Mills, with whom he did not have an appointment.

I was loving L.A. My last visit to California's southern region had been to San Diego to see my Uncle Jimmy and Aunt Fran at 13. Popeye and I didn't take in tourist attractions. We went to everyday spots with real flavor—Spike Lee's Joint, an evening out at a popular nightclub with Popeye's buddy, Jerome Benton, and a late breakfast each day at Roscoe's

Chicken 'N Waffles on Sunset and Gower, a veritable spot-the-stars dining experience. But the most interesting moment fell on the final day.

First, we stopped by Perspective Records so Popeye could check on the marketing and promotion of his boys. Compared to Epic, Columbia, and MCA, Perspective's headquarters were modest. Popeye stuck his head in every office and cubicle we passed, seemingly at home in the West Coast operation. A couple of the folks were kind enough to explain their jobs to me, and, before we left, they filled my arms with an advanced copy of Mint's new video and CD singles of Perspective artists.

We then walked from Perspective to the A&M lot, Perspective's distribution arm, to the office of a woman in the black-music division. She was friendly and chatty, and they discussed a variety of subjects, all music-related, none of more than passing interest, until we prepared to leave. The woman asked Popeye if he was going to "the wedding," and he shrugged and said he hadn't decided. She showed great surprise. Eyes bulged. Jaw dropped. I got the distinct impression she had not been invited, and would have RSVP'd "yes" in a heartbeat if she had. I waited patiently as they ended their meeting, and the minute we were out the door, I asked, "Who's getting married?"

"Jimmy."

"Jimmy who?"

"Jimmy Jam."

"When is it?"

"June 25."

"You mean the end of this month?!"

"Yeah, what's the big deal?"

"Where is it?"

"Beverly Hills."

I couldn't believe it hadn't come up or that he hadn't committed to going, whatever his reasons. I quickly learned he could bring a guest and knew he and his girlfriend weren't on the best of terms, if not already broken up. I saw a gold mine, a once-in-a-lifetime occasion to network among big names in the business. I could pass out business cards, make contacts, and, yes, witness one of the biggest social events of the year. It loomed within my grasp, so close. Popeye needed only to agree to go and to take me.

I had no problem coaxing, cajoling, and just plain working his last nerve. For over four hours of uninterrupted plane time, I asked if he had lost his mind.

"How can you not go? And so, fine, even if *you* don't want to go, what about me?? *You're* the one who suggested I go into this business. Don't you want to help me?"

He assured me if he did go, I could be his guest. He just wasn't sure yet that he would go. He would let me know in a few days.

"But the wedding is in three weeks. I need time to get an advance fare, shop, make hotel arrangements, and shop."

"Kim, I'll tell you in a few days."

He went his way when the plane landed in Minneapolis, and I rode my final leg to Madison, mulling over the possibilities. I decided not to bother him anymore. I simply waited, and not more than a couple of days later, he said it was a go.

I already had cleared it with Bill. I didn't want to do anything to make him uncomfortable and would have stayed home if he had had a problem with my going as Popeye's guest. But having met Popeye and grown comfortable with our friendship, Bill voiced no reservations. My next stop was a return to the office of the administrative partner who had just signed off on the L.A. excursion three weeks before. I explained who Jimmy Jam was (his daughters loved Janet) and why the event was a can't-miss. He understood and signed off again. I left his office eternally grateful.

With green lights from Popeye, Bill, and the administrative partner, the overriding, all-consuming, to-the-point-of-absurd concern became "What should I wear!?"

The dilemma presented challenges I hadn't encountered

for my own wedding. Then, it didn't matter what others wore. It was *my* day. I could dress up or down, traditional or funky, and order others' attire in the party around my choice. This was different. It wasn't my show, my crowd, or my scene. I couldn't fathom what their set would wear to a 5:00 P.M. Beverly Hills wedding. Beads? Sequins? Long? Short? The issue concerned me far more than it should have. I called my mother, my East Coast friends, and contemplated the look of a different world. "Simple black dress" got the vote for safest bet, but as always, I wanted something a little different, something with individual style, without going against the grain.

I had no idea what I was looking for, but I headed to Michigan Avenue, certain I would find it. Between Lord & Taylor's, Marshall Field's, Bloomingdale's, Saks, Neiman Marcus, and every boutique within the Magnificent Mile, I had no doubt I would spot *something*. I was wrong. Nothing excited me. Late in the day, I stood on the corner of Michigan and Pearson, frustrated and discouraged. If I could find nothing there, where on earth would I go? Determined not to leave empty-handed, I backtracked to a boutique that had the most promise, realizing at that point I'd only be settling.

I tried on a cute white dress trimmed in one-inch black fabric at the upper bodice, with thick black straps that crisscrossed in the back. It fit close to the body and stopped just short of the knees. After the saleswoman touted the dress design's good taste and style, I relented. It would have made a statement in any of my circles, but I wasn't traveling in my circle. With one week until show time and Michigan Avenue exhausted, though, I had the dress tailored to my size and exacted a promise of rushed delivery.

I lived with my choice for two days. By Monday I found myself looking around Madison, of all places. I visited the trendiest boutiques in the hopes something extraordinary had found its way there. Nothing had, but I got a tip from a local saleswoman about a designer boutique in Milwaukee called Zita's. That evening I motored down Interstate 94.

When a Zita's saleswoman asked what I was looking for, I told her the particulars of the event, and, with confidence, she sat me in a dressing room and returned with her selection. She chose two pieces, both black, but by different designers. The top was an evening halter, thick and silky. It hugged the top of the neck, anchored by two buttons at the nape, and draped down softly over the torso. The fabric came together generously at the lower back with four buttons, exposing only the upper middle of my spine. The silky skirt, ankle-length and slim-fitting, fit over the halter and flaunted a sharp split up the left leg. I knew immediately that it would work. The saleswoman dashed away again and returned with a thin gold chain, lightly beaded, and flung it around my neck. It hung to the tops of my thighs.

"Do I double it up?" I asked.

"No. Absolutely not. This is the look. It will be beautiful."

The Perspective and Flyte Tyme families gathered at a hotel reception Friday evening, June 24. The patriarchs weren't present, just the production staff from Minnesota, the label staff from California, and some of Perspective's artists. The hotel, secluded and nestled in a quiet residential area in West Hollywood, sat adjacent to Beverly Hills and only a couple of blocks from Sunset Strip. Popeye knew the manager and had gotten us reduced rates for both trips. I had no idea it would serve as headquarters for Flyte Tyme as well. I thought back to four months before, the night of Mint Condition's concert in Milwaukee, when I was "Joe Fan," privy to nothing, no clue whether the performers' caravan had left town or was headed down the road to Best Western. And here I was, staying with them at the same hotel. The vibe was surreal.

The reception was filled with familiar faces, people I had met in Minneapolis and at Perspective a few weeks before. I had great interest in being there but didn't make a point of being present. It wasn't my family, nor was it my intent to get adopted into the family. I knew the quickest way to turn people off, especially women, was to act as if I needed to be part of their world. It wasn't my nature anyway. I made conversation when approached, laughed when appropriate, and otherwise kept my mouth shut and listened. I heard a lot, tidbits about people and goings-on in the industry. And I learned a lot about the people there, which ones had superegos, which ones were friendly, and which ones had nothing going on upstairs.

One impressed me, "Prof T." from the group Lo-Key? He was engaged in a debate with a Perspective staff member about industry "truths," how he could no longer write music for the love, because it had become a job, and his job was to satisfy the dictates of the market. He spoke with passion and inspired input from those around him, including me. He touched on other subjects as well, all in an opinionated fashion but in a very positive way. We built a rapport, mostly by my bouncing issues off him and his responding with thoughtful, definitive views. I would value his knowledge and wisdom about the business in months to come.

Popeye drove around Los Angeles like a native son. He knew shortcuts, side streets, where to glimpse the fabulous views. With the same ease of direction, he drove to the Pickfair Estate and pulled our rented Toyota Camry up to the gate, alongside high and luxury sedans and cameramen who stood at the ready to capture famous faces. Once our names had been duly verified, we were given access onto the grounds and followed a path to the magnificent front entryway.

It had the aura of a palace. My eyes darted by the second, checking out architecture, intricate flooring, stunning floral arrangements, and the next group of people to walk through the entrance. We hung inside for a while as Popeye greeted a cavalcade of stars, and then moved to the outside, where the festivities would take place. The setup was breathtaking, the weather gorgeous.

We secured good seats on the aisle, halfway down from the front. When most everyone had seated themselves, before the bridal procession began, heads turned as an escort led Janet Jackson to a seat up front. She looked beautifully svelte in a slim, sleeveless black dress and sported long braids pulled away from her face. Jimmy Jam and best man Terry stood at the front in champagne-colored tuxedos, Panama hats, and dark shades.

To be sure, it was the bride's day. Lisa Padilla looked every bit the princess in her gorgeous satin gown, but as we all stood to frame her walk down the rose-studded aisle, my attention was helplessly diverted. Babyface and his wife, Tracey, stood across the aisle from us, with Tia Carrera behind them. I recognized Motown Chairman Clarance Avant, Motown President Jheryl Busby, and Hollywood manager Delores Robinson within rows of us. As much as I labored to be nonchalant, I found reason to flex my neck every 10 seconds.

Sounds of Blackness and Lisa Keith sang beautiful wedding-day songs, the bride and groom kissed officially, and mingling on the lawn began in earnest. I thought two and three times about approaching Babyface, who stood no more than five feet from me, just to say, "You're awesome." I knew he wouldn't get a big head, which made the move more attractive, but I had ordered myself to stay on non-fan mode. So I didn't approach him, nor Holly Robinson and Rodney Peete, Quincy Jones, or Cassandra Mills. But one personality I couldn't resist.

I waited until he was alone with his date on the lawn and told him how, as a young teenager, I had written him a letter and he had told me in a return letter to follow my dreams. Donnie Simpson was flabbergasted, gracious, and fun.

Popeye and I gravitated mostly around the Flyte Tyme–associated crew—Jellybean, Jerome, Cherrelle, Johnny Gill, and others. If I talked to people for more than a few minutes, I queried them about whether they had an attorney and found a way to slip them my business card and the information that I practiced entertainment law. I also asked people how they were referred to their attorneys and what they found important about the client-attorney relationship. I got my most direct answer from Janet Jackson.

She had stayed away from the mingling session but sat with her beau, Rene, at the bridal table for dinner. When the guests had dined, the reception became a live concert, starting with Mint Condition performing "Forever in Your Eyes" for the couple's first dance. Sounds of Blackness and Lisa Keith performed again. Lo-Key? and Johnny Gill took the stage. And all throughout, well-wishers with enough clout to step to the bridal table were doing so. It was very accessible, toward the back of the reception area, just off the dance floor. I stood back there as a small crowd formed and watched as Popeye offered his congratulations to the couple and kissed Janet on the cheek. She was seated, and Rene was perched over her in a guard-dog stance. He granted permission with his eyes, and only the inner circle got near her.

I threw in the towel on my non-fan resolution.

"Popeye, ask Rene if I can get a picture with Janet."

"Aw, Kim, come on. You see all these people around here trying to get to her."

"Popeye, seriously. Just ask him. If he says no, then it's just no."

Popeye whispered to him, and Rene looked my way and waved his hand. I sat next to Janet at the bridal table, and she smiled broadly as Popeye snapped our picture. Then, capitalizing on the moment, I said, "Can I ask you a question?"

Janet said, "Sure."

"I'm an attorney trying to break into the entertainment law business, and I know your attorney is Don Passman—I read his book—and I'm wondering how you chose him. What was important to you?"

"Oh . . . Don's here," she said, looking around the room. "Maybe he's gone now. Well, I spoke to many attorneys who all made the same promises and probably could have all done the same things for me. But what was important to me was that I click with my attorney personality-wise, because it's a close working relationship, and I have to be able to trust him."

She was neither shy nor arrogant. She stared in my eyes as she spoke and made me feel she cared to answer my question. I got the total impression she was about her business and knew every detail about the things I had been trying to learn in the past few months.

Sitting and talking to Janet for just five minutes was a bigger deal than my face would have ever showed. She's a superstar, known worldwide, and my getting that close to her symbolized for me how far I could go in the business. But as much a highlight as the Janet encounter was, another topped it. The night was drawing to a close, and I had occasion to speak with Stokley for a few moments. As I began to walk away, he said, "Oh, I found your letter, and that poem. I love poetry. It was beautiful."

I waited to dissolve into the night, assured the fairy tale had reached capacity. My fairy godmother would appear, waving her magic wand, before my eyes only, and zap me back to a lifeless existence in Madison. The day, the year, would fade into oblivion, and I'd never be quite sure whether it was real to begin with. Popeye and I would never share another conversation, the idea of a singing career would again seem patently ludicrous, and I would devote 100 percent of my legal practice, once more, to civil litigation.

That was my nightmare. I had rubbed elbows with the world I admired from afar, and I had no intention of putting space between us. On the flight home, I formulated excited ideas of building my entertainment law practice, anything, to stay in the flow. I wanted to be a player, whether as an artist or as an attorney to an up-and-coming artist or producer, one who would make it big and take me along. If I worked hard and persevered, I had no doubt I could do it, even from the Midwest, even from Madison.

As I thought on it, Madison was integral to the plan. Had I stayed in D.C., I couldn't have driven to Minnesota to meet with Popeye nor experienced the milestones that followed. I was certain that I had discovered my reason for being there. God had worked it all out for me. He knew my dreams and wanted to position me to realize them. I kicked myself for complaining, for being impatient, and thanked God for the doors He had opened. I prayed that I would be successful in the business and continue to build upon the contacts I made. I had found my way into the world I loved, and I had no plans of giving it up.

Part II

After

Chapter 7

⬗

Leaving Darkness

WE STOPPED GOING TO CHURCH. THE SPIRITUAL FERVOR DIED when, month after month, we heard sermons that rarely dealt with life application. They were nice messages, ones that praised God and touched on biblical times, but they left us with nothing to chew on, nothing to think about. We'd drive off having learned little, wondering why we went, and convinced we could do better, or at least as well, on our own. We took to skipping Sundays here and there and fell off entirely in the first part of 1994.

In-home worship took its place. We'd get out Bill's Bible and read a few verses—no discussion, no effort at real understanding—listen to some gospel music, then turn on the NFL pregame show. Our service lasted no more than 15 minutes, and we satisfied ourselves that we had done our Sunday best. In fact, we had maximized our Sundays. We could get the spiritual nourishment we needed without stepping foot in a snow boot or donning a down coat. And we truly believed it was enough until, somewhere deep, we both felt a light tapping on our souls. A small voice insisted, "This ain't gettin' it. Look for another church if you don't want to go back to St. Ann's, but you need to get up out of here."

We talked of looking for a new church, and talked, but by the time we debated where to go and which denomination to try, we'd give up and return to "Let's just worship at home." Months passed with the same routine, and then I returned home from Los Angeles the evening of June 26. Bill met me at the door fully animated, caring not about whom I met at the wedding but about what he had seen and heard that day.

"I visited St. Paul A.M.E. Church this morning. You would not believe the service."

"A.M.E.? How'd you find a black church?"

"My barber, Ben Parks, invited me yesterday. We've been talking about finding a new church, so I went to check it out. Smooch, the pastor was *serious*. I learned more today than I have in the last year at the other church. And the people were real friendly. I joined today. I had to. I was moved."

"You joined without me?"

"I know. I wouldn't have normally, but you'll understand when you go next week."

St. Paul was located in a brick building on a corner lot, two blocks off the downtown square, very near my office. We arrived for the 11:00 A.M. worship service and walked into a sanctuary much smaller than St. Ann's. The warmth struck me right off. People left conversations with others to shake our hands with broad smiles and welcome "Brother Tate" back, and me to St. Paul for the first time.

The scene put a different face on Madison. Black people of all ages gathered under one roof regularly, a community I hadn't realized existed. I suppose if I were church-minded or cared to think long about anything happening in Madison, common sense would have announced the reality. But for three years it had escaped me. I wondered where they lived and worked and how they coped with existing in a city as white as Madison.

We sat in a pew near the back, and I watched Pastor George Thomas walk to the pulpit in his unadorned black robe. He had the build of a man nearing his midfifties, slightly paunchy, and stood about five feet eight inches tall. The pastor raised his arms for the congregation to stand, and the choir director played a lively piano as the choir marched in, singing, with a quick step. I perused my program for the order of service, wondering, admittedly, how long we'd be there. Bill had said the service lasted no more than two hours, which was double the Catholic service, but doable. I wasn't up for an all-day affair, and I had heard some churches tended that way.

The pastor knew his members' names and called on them at random to do scripture readings, to invite people to the altar for prayer, and to lead the testimony. Of all the worship items, save for the sermon, the testimonies roused my spirit the greatest. People stood and, one by one, expressed publicly how God had blessed them with personal victories, from waking them up that morning to safe travel out of town and back, to solving worrisome problems. Some spoke reservedly, others full of excitement, but all with solid assurance that God had worked in their lives and was worthy to be praised. To me, their testifying couldn't have been more forceful had they taken the stand in a courtroom downtown and sworn an oath; the conviction of their hearts spoke louder than any promise to tell the truth. But as credibly as they fulfilled their witness role, I could lay no claim to my weekday role of trial lawyer. As the lawyer, I would know the facts of the case backward and forward, having done my homework for as many days, nights, and weekends as it took to master them. Certainly I would have a better grasp than the witnesses, whose knowledge would extend to the length of a puzzle piece. But I wasn't up on the case of praise and worship. At St. Paul, the witnesses were educating me. I took the low seat and listened up.

Together, the church read from the gospel of St. John, the scripture from which the pastor would preach, then the choir sang its third song, and the pastor came down from the pulpit to bring the message. He eased into it, talking first about life issues we all could identify with. When he got us on board, he moved to the scripture text, breaking it down verse by verse, word by word at times, until the meaning was plain. And then he served up the meat, driving home the relevance of the scripture text to the very life issues he had raised up front. The substance of his message penetrated, helped no doubt by the style of his delivery. He wasn't there to entertain—no rocking on the heels, jumping up and down, or infusing words with melodious pitches. He injected humor here and there, but, for the most part, he was serious like Bill said. He didn't coddle the congregation or reshape the Word to soothe the masses. He told it like it was: how we should live, the attitudes we needed to embrace, the behaviors we needed to drop. And he said it with all the aura of a leader, speaking deliberately, in a tone that commanded respect, never slouching in articulation, never wavering in the face of a difficult point.

My soul had been waiting to be fed. It gobbled Pastor Thomas's words and soared to dizzying heights. I heard it lobbying, "This is it! This is what we've needed!" I didn't quarrel. I saw it for myself. The pastor had overturned the rock I'd been living under and handed me a rude awakening. God expected me to behave a certain way, feel a certain way, and I lived far from the ideal. I knew it, not once bothering to dismiss his message or delude myself. The truth had chased me down and cornered me right in St. Paul. I received it defeatedly and acknowledged I had much to learn. I was ready to learn. And Pastor Thomas was, by far, the best teacher ever to cross my path.

The congregation stood at the close of the sermon and sang a hymn as the pastor invited visitors to join the church. Bill and I exchanged looks, and I whispered my intentions. I began walking toward the front of the aisle and heard *Amens* from the pews and people clapping. The pastor said, "Brother Tate, come join your wife," and Bill took to my side.

The church secretary wrote down my name, address, and the A.M.E. church in which I had been baptized and presented me to the pastor. Pastor Thomas smiled, shook my hand, and asked, "Sister Tate, do you believe in the Lord Jesus

Christ as the Son of God and Savior of the world?" Without hesitation, I replied, "Yes." He welcomed me into the St. Paul family and invited the congregation to give me "the right hand of welcome." Pews emptied, and person after person filed by, extending hands, hugs, and lots of *God-bless-yous*.

Tears hung just beneath the surface. My head throbbed, not from pain but from the weight of self-imposed shame and embarrassment over not taking the step sooner. Where have I been? I thought. All of these people had been at St. Paul week after week learning, and growing, while I played church at home, learning nothing. I could feel an internal shift occurring, a changing of the guard, as my low-key spirituality assumed front and center and placed me firmly at the foot of a long and winding path. I had no clue what I needed for the journey, no clue what to expect, no clue how to endure. But in the distance I could see a light shimmering magnificently enough that even I at the outskirts could share in its brilliance. I knew too well the darkness that loomed a few feet behind, and I didn't look back.

Pastor Thomas loves the Lord Jesus. He talks up Jesus, emphasizes Jesus, and not a Sunday passes when he doesn't speak about his admiration. He often talked about the gifts Jesus had given, how He had left His heavenly kingdom to enter this sinful world as a man, how He put up with scorn, rejection, and ridicule and then died a slow, cruel death so we might be saved. Like a child eulogizing a beloved parent, the pastor got filled up when he reflected on these things. He stressed the debt of gratitude we owed Jesus, how we could never repay Him but how, daily, we ought thank Him and show our love.

I didn't love Jesus. Without much of a relationship to speak of, I couldn't profess an emotion as strong as "love." He was God, certainly. Powerful. All-knowing. But He was out there in the heavens, not in my heart. I didn't talk about Him or talk much to Him and didn't know a whole lot about His life and times on Earth. It was weird admitting how little I knew, having believed in His Deity for so long. But belief had gotten me only so far, and there I was at the age of 27, believing and ignorant. I knew the law, and various social theories thrown at me in college, but had never studied even one of Jesus' parables. And the things I was familiar with, such as the crucifixion and the resurrection, meant nothing to me on a personal level. I welled up quickly over sappy movies but, past that third-grade Easter, felt little sadness when reminded of Jesus' death. It was a historical fact, far removed in time and far removed from my emotions.

But I listened week after week to the pastor and heard how joyous Jesus made him. I saw how fired-up Jesus made him. And I saw how much trust he put in Jesus. The congregation was small, fewer than 100 regular attendees, but the pastor refused bake sales and chicken-dinner fund-raisers. "Jesus said, 'My Father's house shall *not* be a house of merchandise,'" the pastor would declare. "We won't sell a single chicken leg here. God will provide."

I wanted to make the pastor's Jesus my Jesus. I wanted the kind of relationship he had cultivated with God, though I doubted my ability to do it. My highest levels of love and trust extended to my mother and to Bill, but the pastor was talking something altogether different. Something boundless and superior, a wholesale harnessing of heart, soul, and mind. I didn't give that much of myself, never had, but had also never felt that measure of the pastor's joy. I made up my mind to get to know God, and I began the process with prayer. Real communal prayer.

I used a model handed out by the pastor and, over time, added on. It opened not with "I need" or "Please bless me with" but with "Thank you." "Thank you, heavenly Father, for sending us your only Son. . . . Thank you, Lord Jesus, for suffering for us. . . . Thank you, Lord, for the gift of your Holy Spirit and your holy Word. . . ."

It addressed spiritual needs—the need for the Holy Spirit to lead, guide, and direct me and the need for God's Word to make, shape, and mold me into a person with whom He could be pleased. Once I had given thanks and prayed for spiritual betterment, I moved to fleshly desires, like being successful in the music business. And I began closing my prayers, ". . . In the name of Jesus I pray. Amen." The pastor had reminded the congregation (and told me for the first time) that Jesus had said to ask in His name and it would be given unto us. "Don't send your mail up to heaven without any postage," the pastor warned. I've stamped mine ever since.

I felt good when I prayed. At first. The bridge I had built between God and myself toppled slightly with each heartfelt consultation. I was reaching out and felt Him grabbing hold. But one day, without my sensing its arrival, Discontent found me, even in prayer, and tried pulling me back. It used recurring images, which invaded my prayers. I'd find myself kneeling in palatial quarters opulent with gold and precious stones and bright with heavenly light. Before me, high up on a wondrous throne, sat God the Father and the Lord Jesus, though I dared not look. With my head bowed humbly, I'd open my mouth to address God in prayer, and, as if on cue, my multitude of sins would dance like neon signs before Him. I could see each distracting one and felt ugly in His sight, undeserving of His time and attention. I wanted to run away but prayed anyway, with nagging images in tow.

The pastor helped ease my guilt with one word. Repentance. As if reading my mind, he spoke on it in depth one day, called it "The Three Rs." "Realize your mistakes. Regret that you made them. And resolve not to do them again." If our hearts were sincere, he said, God would wipe the slate clean. I reflected on it all evening. Jesus had died for *me*, so *my* sins would be forgiven, and all I had to do was claim it. It was incredible.

With a heavy heart, I reflected on the past, especially of my time at Maryland. Alice. Nicole. The vulgar behavior. The immoral behavior. Memory after memory pervaded my mind, and I received each with grief and asked God's forgiveness. For days I remained sad, appalled actually, over what I had been. I couldn't move beyond. And then I looked to God, who lifted the fog so I could see Discontent for what it was. I didn't have to torture myself. I didn't have to let guilt impede a closer walk with God. If He could forgive me, I could forgive myself. I turned a corner that day, burying the old self and setting my mind to molding the new.

Within two months, Bill and I were changing, not by leaps and bounds overnight but with a steady, plodding shift. We didn't think about skipping church. We stopped peppering our conversations with curse words and attributing our circumstances, good or bad, to "luck" . . . though I learned the latter the hard way.

I stood in church to give one of my first testimonies, happily learning to give God the glory, and pronounced loudly that I was "lucky" to have had some great thing befall me. No one commented, but a few eyebrows raised, and when I sat down, Bill said, "*Blessed*. You're blessed to have had that happen. Christians don't believe in 'luck.'"

"God's will" replaced "fate." "God's plan" did away with a need to read horoscopes. And "God's mercy" supplanted any reference to "I deserve" or "I'm worthy." But as marked a change as two months wrought, I didn't read the Bible, didn't even have my own, and I wasn't taking advantage of group study at the church. I felt no compulsion to stretch my attendance beyond Sundays from 11:00 to 1:00. I already had increased my worship time by nearly 500 percent and, as a result, regularly missed the NFL pregame show and half of the game. I was pleased with the pace of my progress—a somewhat easy, comfortable crawl down the Christian path—and could not have anticipated the shake-up lying around the bend.

Chapter 8

---◆---

Temptation

THE MINUTE I HEARD REMY SING, I KNEW SHE WAS SOMETHING special. Confident, she chose a Toni Braxton hit and stepped into it as if Babyface had penned it for her, kicking a smooth, smoldering alto more beautiful than most I'd heard. Then she upped the range and her audacity with a rendition of Whitney Houston's "I Will Always Love You" and more than held her own, all in an informal, over-the-phone introduction.

"I told you she was bad," Steve said in a wide-smiling voice.

"I'm telling you. You go, girl!"

Steve Cooper and Remy Frazier had grown up in the same Massachusetts town, and he professed to be her biggest fan. More than once, she had tasted a big break. The biggest "almost" came when she replaced the lead singer of a one-hit-wonder female group and toured with them across the country. The exposure led to an offer of a recording contract to sing on the second album, which ultimately died when the parties couldn't come to terms. She was 27 now, my age, wisely working a nine-to-five job and mulling over another contract put before her. Steve, whom I met during law school, knew of my dabbling in the business and recommended she talk to me. Their call came one summer evening in 1994, with Steve in Maryland and Remy in Atlanta.

Steve hung up after providing introductions and background, and Remy talked specifics as to the deal presented her. A production team wanted to sign her, and one of the team's principals, an attorney, had offered to represent her. She smelled a conflict and wanted independent advice, admitting up front she couldn't afford my hourly rate but desirous of paying something nonetheless. I told her not to worry about it, that we'd settle up when she hit it big.

Remy faxed me the contract at work the next day. I reviewed it and questioned her more about the people involved. They were unproven, and their prospects for taking her to the next level were suspect, yet they sought to tie her to them for a number of years. Neither of us was thrilled, but she didn't know whether another opportunity would come her way. Very soon thereafter, though, one did.

Remy called excited one day. She'd been invited by a girlfriend to a party at the home of a woman interested in finding talent for a record label. When she told me the woman's name—Faye Baxter—I joined in Remy's excitement at once and told her about my quick meeting with Ms. Baxter and the little I knew about the project she had in the works. We discussed what Remy should wear to the party and, if the opportunity arose, what she should sing. She promised to call me at home Saturday morning with all details. The phone rang *early*.

She was ecstatic. Remy had gone to this woman's party and turned it out, singing song after song with a captivated audience gathered around her. Faye was so taken that she pulled Remy into her bedroom, gave her some fancy clothes and jewelry to wear, and filmed her performance to show others. She hinted she might be in touch with Remy regarding a recording contract, and Remy's hopes had spiraled through the roof.

In the weeks following, Faye seemed to adopt Remy as

her protégée. She invited Remy to her beautiful home a few more times and took to calling her now and then to see how she was doing. Sounding more assured, Faye spoke of this contract she hoped to present Remy but said she needed others above her to approve her choice. Remy and I grew more anxious by the day. At her request, I called Faye, reintroduced myself, and told her I'd be representing Remy if and when an offer unfolded. Faye remembered me, expressed enthusiasm over Remy's talent, and said she'd be in touch.

Remy and I conversed often, sometimes two or more times per day, as she shared developments or excitement over what could be. We got along well. She had an easygoing personality and a hilarious sense of humor . . . well, she was crazy, quick to fall into uproarious laughter over her own, admittedly funny witticisms. I enjoyed her, and when it appeared a deal might be in the offing, I decided to meet Remy in person to cement my new attorney-client relationship.

I flew to Atlanta near summer's end, and Remy met me at the airport, looking nothing like I had expected. Her speaking voice was as rich as her singing, grand and full of flavor. But in person stood this five-foot-four-inch, very petite woman, seemingly powerless to belt out the kind of sound I had heard by phone. She had beautiful brown skin and medium-length hair, and she flashed a warm smile the second we recognized each other. I said to myself, "This here is a star."

We spent the weekend eating out, talking, and just hanging at Remy's apartment. We had a great time, never running short on conversation or growing tired of each other's face. She didn't appear to grow tired either of my asking her to sing. I wanted to know the breadth of her range and vocal abilities, and as I listened to her in person, and on old demo tapes she played for me, I concluded simply that she was phenomenal. Without question, her talent exceeded much of what the market had to offer, and I hoped greatly that she would make it, not for any benefit it might bring me but because she had the hands-down, sho-nuff gift.

In fact, after listening to Remy, I abandoned completely my own pursuit of a recording contract. The thought had been brewing for some time after I realized that, in addition to recording an album—the fun part—I'd have to also promote it, likely singing in smoky dives and low-budget venues from city to city, constantly away from my husband. The picture held little appeal, and I had even stopped taking vocal lessons. But Remy sealed it. I had no business striving for a deal when someone with far superlative talent hadn't landed one. I was okay; she was special. And I had no problem acknowledging the difference. I focused my skills on contracts and negotiation and let her be about the business of singing for a living.

We stepped into fall without a contract in hand from Faye's camp. We had heard promises of promises, built hopes on top of hopes, but nothing materialized. Faye's phone calls to Remy faded, as did Remy's belief that this might be it. Word in Atlanta circles had it that the label deal fell through, but whatever happened, Remy again had not much to look forward to but getting up and going to a job she couldn't wait to quit. I felt bad for her, and we continued to talk every so often, but by the end of the year, contact fizzled to nothing.

Nineteen-ninety-five marked several turning points for me, all related in some way to St. Paul. Sunday school provided the catalyst, once I decided to go. My curiosity was piqued (and guilt stirred) when I heard testimonies in morning worship about what a blessing the Sunday school lesson had been or when the pastor referred to an interesting subject covered that morning in the Sunday school. I'd regret missing the discussion, as did Bill, and one Saturday night we agreed to set the clock an hour earlier. The following morning we moved to the next phase of our Christian development.

The dynamic was very different from morning worship.

The adult class met in the sanctuary, and everyone sat on the right side of the pews with sheets of paper in hand. The pastor, in a suit but without his robe, walked up and down the aisle, teaching a lesson he himself had conceived, typed up on the computer, and printed out. As I would find, his lessons incorporated a few verses of scripture each week—he was in the gospel of St. Mark the Sunday we started—and he moved sequentially through the Bible to relay better understanding.

I immediately appreciated the Sunday school as highly conducive to learning. The pastor spoke for a longer time, about a variety of issues, and welcomed questions from the congregation, all in an effort to move us to a closer walk with God. To my delight, he didn't mind straying from the written piece and often tackled current events, a recent happening in the church, or a topic raised by one of the members, in a straight-up, forthright manner. His knowledge of the Bible ran deep, and he believed in citing scriptural examples as bases for his opinions. I relished the opportunity to partake of his spiritual wisdom and often asked basic questions to build up my understanding. He was patient with me and tried to make clear that which was not readily apparent.

My spirit thrived on Sunday school nourishment, but the more I learned, the more I knew how much I didn't know. We studied St. Mark, and the pastor preached from St. John in morning worship, but the balance of the Bible remained a mystery to me. I hadn't begun home study and wasn't real confident in my ability to understand if I did. But a desire grew for additional Christian instruction nevertheless, and I was led to get it from Marilyn Parks

Marilyn was the brightest light to shine on me at St. Paul. She directed all of St. Paul's choirs; sang mighty, almost operatic solos; led the Sunday school as superintendent; and, in all that she did, walked with a beautiful, full smile and an unparalleled glow about her. Always upbeat, always superfriendly, always taking the lead, and always the Christian role model, Marilyn seemed unreal. I concluded she was an angel, delivered with God's blessing to the doorstep of my life. She embraced Bill and me, literally, from the moment we joined St. Paul and, once she learned we had no relatives in the area, volunteered to be our "Madison Mom." And meant it. Though she had four 20-something children of her own, her heart accommodated us both (and many others). She called with encouraging words, listened with great interest to the smallest of our cares, and hardly ever accepted personally the *thank-yous* we heaped upon her. "Praise the Lord," she'd say. "Give God the glory!"

Early on I read the announcement in the church program: "Christian Women Supporting Women meets on Wednesday evenings at 5:00 P.M. These confidential meetings encourage spiritual growth, Christian problem solving, and fellowship. You do not have to be a member of St. Paul to participate. See Sister Marilyn Parks, Worship Leader, for information."

"Support" struck me as help for down-and-out problems with alcohol, drugs, or inability to find work, none of which concerned me. I was fine, able to do for myself, and certainly didn't need any crisis intervention. So I glossed over the announcement for months until I was moved one day to ask Marilyn what it was about. She told me Bible study was the focus, and I decided a Marilyn-led study was definitely worth a look-see.

I walked through St. Paul's doors midweek for the first time and into the church lounge, where Marilyn and one other woman were reading from the Bible. No one had ever attended Christian Women on a regular basis. Most weeks Marilyn had sat alone, ready to instruct, waiting for warm bodies.

I joined in the study as Marilyn took her time explaining King James language and making sure we understood every message there was to be had. Like the pastor, her uncle, Marilyn speaks with perfect articulation, crisp and to the point and, also like the pastor, keeps her Christian responsibility uppermost in her mind. Her knowledge of the Bible, how to read it and understand it, illuminated my ignorance. I was on full pupil mode, soaking in every considered word that passed her lips.

My job, far from nine-to-five, precluded me from showing up each week. I attended the following week, and perhaps the next, but missed a few thereafter. When I returned, the original woman was gone (and would not return), and Bridget Thomas sat studying with Marilyn. Bridget had married the pastor's son, Tobin, in October 1994, and joined the church afterward, becoming our only faithful Caucasian member.

By standard measure, this African-American woman from the D.C. area would be hard-pressed to find commonalities enough to bond with a white woman from Wisconsin. But with Bridget I would learn the power of the Christian bond. We were embarking on a parallel journey, both of us babies in the faith, and we had chosen the Christian Women's group as one of our vehicles. Each week our thirst for Christian growth increased, and each week we quenched it in our intimate setting. Starting with Genesis, Marilyn led our march through the Old Testament and happily paused at each verse that prompted a question. Our aim was to understand not just its meaning in *that* day but its meaning in present day and what we needed to do to incorporate it in our lives. After Bible study came open discussion, at which time we could raise any issue under the sun, have it examined from a Christian perspective, and be assured the conversation would never leave the room. And no meeting ended without prayer and testimonies of God's goodness.

The Wednesday association spilled over into other days of the week. Bridget and I began lingering after church on Sunday and talking on the phone, often about issues relative to our Christian growth. I found myself preferring conversation with Bridget over long-distance communications with people back home. I enjoyed talking with my old friends but felt the divide widening each time they spewed curse words or shared sexual, unmarried exploits. They reminded me of where I'd been, an abyss I didn't want to fall back into.

I realized how much I needed the group, my original self-assessment having been way off the mark. I wasn't a recovering alcoholic or drug abuser, but I was recovering from 27 years of darkness, 27 years of worldly influence. I needed support to keep from relapsing, support to remind me that I wasn't in the struggle alone, support to discern the right way. And that Christian support was right there in the summer of 1995 when I began steering a wrong course.

I called Remy early that spring for an update on her musical affairs. Nothing was happening, and I could hear the usually bubbly Remy beginning to despair. Her chief concern, the lack of a current demo tape, seemed an insurmountable yet unavoidable obstacle. She had no one to provide her with music, nor enough money to pay for music and studio time, which can run into the thousands. I wanted to help. Her talent was too great to waste, and I said as much to Popeye as I solicited his assistance. He had music and a studio and, on the strength of our friendship, agreed to Remy's recording of two songs for free. But she had to get there. So I called Steve, who owned his own mortgage lending company, and offered him an opportunity to help pave his favorite singer's road to stardom. He had his travel agent book Remy a ticket to Minneapolis.

I drove and met Remy at the airport one Friday afternoon in May. By Saturday evening, she had recorded a ballad and an up-tempo song, including all the background and harmonies on both. We left on Sunday with a rough copy of the tape, understanding it would take Popeye time to mix the songs, an electronic process in which vocals and instrumentals are adjusted and blended to achieve maximum sound. We needed more songs, though, at least a total of four or five, so I called the next logical person who could hook us up with some music: Eric Long.

Eric and I had kept in contact periodically over the years, and he had made moves in the industry, managing producers and a signed recording act, among other things. I told him I had a singer with awesome talent who needed a demo tape and detailed my association with Remy up to that point. Having heard countless tales of people with "awesome talent" who really couldn't cut the mustard, he wasn't bowled over with enthusiasm. But he had recommendations for me nonetheless—a producer named Terry Lewis (no kidding) and a production duo called K.O. Productions, both based in D.C. K.O. had remixed Monica's "Don't Take It Personal," which was in heavy rotation on D.C. radio, and produced the opening theme on BET's *Teen Summit*, which was playing that summer.

Eric gave me their numbers, and I introduced myself to Terry and Brian Overton, the O in K.O., and discussed with each what we needed and, more importantly, what it would cost. I hung up convinced Remy would have a demo with just two songs. I knew she didn't have the kind of money they were talking. And as far in her corner as I had found myself, I didn't have the wherewithal to back her financially. (Even if I did, Bill would have flashed the detour sign.) But I did have a thought. I called Steve once again and asked how serious he was about helping to pave that road. He had indicated a willingness, but committing to a plane ticket hurt far less than songs and studio time.

Steve surprised me with his offer. He said he believed in Remy enough to pay for whatever it took to complete her promotional package, including photographs and travel. He wanted to be businesslike about it, though, and preferred to work through me. He asked that I consider signing on as her personal manager. Popeye and Eric had inquired much the same, assuming I had taken on the role, given my active involvement. I had no interest in the management route, nor time to make it work. But since three people had raised the issue, it stuck to my brain.

Both Popeye and Eric suggested I didn't have to do *everything*. Once Remy got signed and took off, we could hire a co-manager to travel with her and deal with on-site problems while I cared for Remy Inc. back home—paperwork, contracts, phone conferences, day-to-day advice. Remy and I discussed the idea at length. She felt comfortable with me handling her affairs but, having had a manager before, made it clear she needed one available to her at all times. If I intended to start a management company for several aspiring artists, all clamoring for my time, she wasn't interested. I assured her I wasn't either and that if I did it at all, I'd be opening up shop just for her.

We decided a trial period would benefit us both. I drafted a limited-duration personal manager agreement, told her to have it reviewed by an independent attorney, and in early summer we made it official. Steve and I signed an agreement as well, one that said he would provide me with all the funds necessary to complete Remy's package. If she made money as a recording artist, I would pay him 10 percent of funds earned under my management agreement with her. If she never made it, I wouldn't owe Steve a cent.

Remy and I were of course thrilled with the arrangement. We moved full speed ahead, reserving studio time at K.O. Productions for the first part of June. Terry and Brian sent me tapes with "fat" music tracks that needed lyrics. Remy preferred to write all the lyrics herself, but we didn't have much time between receipt of the tapes and our trip to D.C. So Remy and I collaborated on one song, she wrote two, I wrote two, and a friend of hers in Atlanta wrote one. I wore many hats. Remy and I joked that I was her attorney, manager, co-writer, and, if need be, backup singer.

Daddy and Joyce were hosting one of their holiday cookouts for Memorial Day weekend, and Bill and I had planned for some time to attend and throw down on homemade rolls. While there, we visited K.O. Productions, located very near the Treetop Condominiums, where I grew up. Eric met us at K.O. and introduced us to Brian and Brian's partner, Khalid. The facilities impressed me. They had two full-track studios and an outer office with sofas and chairs to accommodate weary artists enduring late-night recording sessions. I told Brian he'd be pleasantly surprised by Remy's talent and by the speed with which she works. Like Eric, he responded suspiciously, and I couldn't wait for them to see for themselves.

Remy flew into D.C. a couple of weeks later, courtesy of Steve, and stayed at my father's house. We hung out at Jasper's that Friday evening with Steve and sorors, but Saturday we got down to business. We had a goal to record six songs in one weekend. The two recorded in Minneapolis hadn't turned out as well as expected—Remy's voice sounded louder on some parts of songs than in others—so we were back to the drawing board. Brian, Eric, and Terry met Remy for the first time, and we told them which songs we had chosen. Of Brian's, the more expensive, Remy planned to record two, both of them funky, mid-tempo jams. She would record four of Terry's, two ballads and two pop-oriented, mid-tempo grooves. We decided to start with Brian's.

Brian moved to the boards and cued up the music. When he was set, Remy stepped into the vocal booth and began laying down the chorus for the song on which we collaborated, "Settle Down." When her voice boomed through the speakers, Brian, Eric, and Terry looked at one another, looked at me, and focused more intently on Remy. What began as a perfunctory studio session turned quickly to something promising and exciting. The consensus among the fellas: she was *bad*. She wowed them with the richness of her voice, her range, and her ability to hear four-part harmonies in her head and lay them down. They liked the lyrics we had written as well and couldn't believe how rapidly she moved through the songs. She didn't need umpteen takes and, many times, hit it the first go-round. Often we'd look around the room and ask if anyone thought a line could be sung better; the answer, often, was "Nope."

I was a kid in a candy store. I sat at the boards next to Brian (and Terry when we did his songs) and helped produce Remy's vocals, particularly on the songs I had written. I knew where emotion, inflections, and ad-libs lived in the songs and sang them for her so she could sing them better. I was excited, more excited than if I were the one recording. Remy had a real chance, and others in the room developed that sense as much as I had in the preceding months. In fact, as the weekend progressed, the room got more and more crowded as others stopped in to listen to this five-foot-four-inch wonder, no doubt tipped by Brian and Eric. Daddy even came through with a music-buff friend of his, having been inspired by a performance for him and Joyce at the house. And, of course, Steve dropped in periodically to check on his investment.

Steve had insisted he wanted no part in the nuts and bolts of our activities. He would shell out the funds, get updates, and otherwise stay out of the picture. But he stopped by the first time out of "curiosity," then a second time for no stated reason, and, on the third, just kind of hung out. I really wondered what was up when I saw him speaking earnestly with Eric, asking questions about the music business and trying to get a handle on the dollars involved. I chalked it up to a businessman's inquisitiveness but filed it away in the back of my mind.

Everyone but Remy and me expressed surprise over her finishing six songs by Sunday evening. She rolled through them, her voice tiring naturally near the end but finding force enough to wrap it up. We celebrated and lounged in the studio, listening over and over to a tape of all the songs Remy had recorded. The rough, unmixed copy sounded fantastic, and we were high off the possibilities. For me, hearing live versions of our own creations, bare lyrics brought to blossom with such fullness and beauty, was a dream come true. Brian and Terry felt excitement of their own, having had their music dressed up in top-notch vocal finery. Eric had visions, too, thinking of label contacts who might be interested in Remy and the finder's fee he would snag as a result. And then there was Remy, exhausted, voice strained, but delirious with joy. She was the belle of the ball, having wormed her infectious personality into Brian's, Terry's, and Eric's hearts within one weekend. They believed she would succeed, and the consensus said "Settle Down" would be the hit.

Remy and I wanted mixed versions of all the songs, "Settle Down" especially, by the Jack the Rapper Convention, which was being held on July 15 in Atlanta. Jack the Rapper had become the place for aspiring artists to make industry contacts, and though Remy's package hadn't been completed, we planned to show up and peddle our tape to as many as would listen.

Brian mixed his songs in time. He tweaked "Settle Down" by adding new instrumental sounds and constructing an even funkier intro. On "Feel the Heat" he did much the same but also included in the bridge a sample from rapper Biz Markie. We loved the product and entered the convention hall optimistic and looking for opportunity. Not much surfaced. By all accounts, industry turnout was dismal. I did catch Louis Bell, president of Orlando-based Rip-It Records, after a panel discussion in which he participated, and asked him to listen. He put on our Walkman headphones and seemed genuinely enchanted. He asked who was singing, I pointed to Remy, and he gave me his number with instructions to get in touch. I also ran into So So Def president Jermaine Dupree, who was too busy to listen on the spot but handed me his card and told me to call. I would try reaching both in the weeks to follow, to no avail.

We made the most of Jack the Rapper nonetheless, attending seminars, watching newly signed acts perform, and assuring ourselves that the following year, Remy wouldn't be walking convention halls without heads turning in her wake.

I remained a student of the business, reading whatever I could get my hands on and taking advantage of human resources. As managers, Eric and Popeye possessed helpful information, but I wanted artists' perspectives of good management and turned to two at my disposal.

I picked Prof T's brain most, extracting experiences and opinions, which he willingly shared for my edification. Stokley was forthcoming as well. Mint had changed management, and he explained the qualities he valued in Popeye as well as in Mint's new manager, industry veteran Larkin Arnold.

They also did me the favor of listening to Remy's mixed demo tape. Prof deemed it "okay"—which provoked a charge of his having incredibly eccentric musical taste—but Stokley returned positive reviews. The informal poll had no bearing on my outlook. Luther Vandross got booed several times off the Apollo Theater stage in his amateur beginning. Had Prof and Stokley hated Remy, I would have stayed on task.

With the demo done, we moved to Remy's image. She wanted a sophisticated, sexy image, and we'd been looking through magazines and in stores when I visited, intending to buy a few outfits and have pictures taken in them. But Eric proposed an alternative, a meeting in New York with Angelo Ellerbee, President of Double XXposure. Double XXposure specializes in image making, publicity, and management and worked with platinum artists such as Mary J.

Blige. Eric considered Angelo a friend, and, in a three-way conference call, we arranged a date for Remy and me to sit down with him.

Remy and I stayed at the Rihga Royal hotel, on 54th Street in midtown Manhattan, down the block from Double XXposure. We met the effusive Mr. Ellerbee, who proceeded to school us on the business of image making and the importance of artists making a positive impression in magazine and television interviews. He told us stories of 'round-the-way artists, whom he taught to hold their own in the limelight, and showed us portfolios that chronicled the development of artists' images.

He said Double XXposure could collaborate with Remy on her image and then set up a photo shoot complete with wardrobe, hairstylists, and makeup artists. The concept excited us, but we needed a cost estimate, which he couldn't give before we left.

I warned Steve it might be expensive, and my suspicions were confirmed . . . more thousands of dollars. He didn't refuse to send it but didn't wire the money right away either. Remy and I got worried. Momentum had been building since the recording session, and the pictures represented the last hurdle before shopping the complete package. If Steve said no to Double XXposure, we'd go to plan B, but we needed an answer.

Against his word, Steve inserted himself in the process, wanting to haggle with Double XXposure, questioning their expertise and asking too many times whether they were worth the money. Then he started second-guessing our overall plans on the basis of his limited knowledge of the business and offering up alternatives that made little sense. He plain got on my nerves, and I began wondering whether our arrangement would withstand his antics when he pulled a surprise plan C out of his hat.

"I'm thinking about starting an independent label here

in D.C. I've been talking to some people, and I think it could work. But I just want to be behind-the-scenes, the financial backer. I won't do it unless you agree to head it up as president. And maybe Eric would be willing to come on board, too."

The pitch appealed to me, but I needed far more information. Eric (who was indeed interested), Steve, and I had numerous conference calls just hammering out the obstacles we faced, the major one being the huge influx of money Steve needed from a business deal that had not yet culminated. We talked distributors, people to add to our team, financial projections, street promotion, and a myriad of other topics. Eric and I made additional calls to people in the industry and took copious notes regarding each step to bringing the project to fruition. And I talked to Bill, who bordered on approval of the idea and thought he could at least make some calls about returning to the University of Maryland.

Remy screamed when I told her the possibilities. She had no qualms about signing with a new label whose energy would be targeted totally to promoting her as its star. We all believed she would be a hit out of the box and were committed to making it happen. Eric and I discussed additional acts we would need to round out the label, but, without a doubt, Remy would be our centerpiece.

The more tangible the idea became, the more attractive it seemed: Steve fronts the money. I move back home. Head of a label. Player in the industry. I saw myself mixing it up, calling the shots, living the ultimate music-lover's fantasy. I thought my prayers had been answered.

Temptation is a close cousin to Discontent. They both work to distance us from God, but Temptation is slicker. It's not always about the blatant—orchestrating private meetings between a single man and married woman and igniting forbidden passion between them. Temptation thrives on the subtle as well, the seemingly innocuous. . . .

I shared my "good news" with Marilyn that I might be moving back to D.C. to help launch and head up a record label. She was at my house, and my mother, in town for a visit, piped in her concerns about the venture not being "practical." I had heard it before and immediately turned defensive.

"If God is blessing me with this, 'practicalities' are irrelevant. I'll work hard and have faith that He'll see me through." In defensive moments, I enjoyed invoking God with my mother, knowing she still didn't know Him and couldn't relate to a higher level of existence.

Marilyn asked what responsibilities I would have. Happily, I described what I knew and she interspersed *I-see*s and *Okay*s but otherwise reserved comment . . . until the following day.

I heard urgency in her voice when I answered the phone. "Kim, I want to talk to you about this record label. I was on my knees in prayer last night about it, and it became clear to me. Satan is trying to tempt you away from all of the progress you've been making as a Christian. You've been attending Sunday school and Bible studies, and you're faithful to the Christian Women's group, and he *does not like it*. He knows how much you love music, and he's put this opportunity before you. But you'll be accountable to God for everything this label puts out on the market—lyrics and images—and I see this thing being nothing but trouble."

"But why would I be accountable for songs and images the label's artists come up with?" I asked sincerely.

"Because you'd be head of the label. And whatever the label's name appears on will reflect on you. When we stand in the judgment, we will be held accountable for everything. And if you've been party to placing immoral lyrics and images on the market, you'll have to answer for it."

"Do you really think so?"

"I'm convinced of it. I know you don't want to hear this, but I wouldn't tell you if I didn't love you."

When Marilyn and I finished, I went upstairs, lay across my bed, and cried. Bill came up to see what happened. When he heard Marilyn's words, he recognized them as wisdom, as did I, which is why it hurt. My mother's "Don't do it" was easily dismissed, but Marilyn's caution was of a different sort. She was steeped in Christ and, I was certain, had a pipeline to God. He was speaking through her just as surely as He had placed her, with a purpose, in my life.

As difficult as it was, I wanted to do the right thing. I wanted God's approval. Certainly, I didn't want to be used by satan, whom I had come to recognize as the author of Temptation *and* Discontent. If he had the gall to tempt Jesus, I had no doubt he would pursue a lightweight like me, and I hated the idea of giving him the victory. With a heavy heart, I backed away.

I called Remy first. After all we'd been through, as far as we'd come, I hated to let her down. I explained that I was trying to live a Christian life, which she knew, and that the label would run counter to my growth.

Surprisingly, Remy, not a Christian, said, "I can understand what you're saying. But if the label is a problem, isn't it also a problem for you to manage me? I mean, some of the songs have sexual overtones—and you know they're not referring to married people—and I do want this sexy image. Won't these things be problems for you, too?"

"I guess you're right. I hadn't thought that much into it . . . but I guess you're right." I sounded depressed, like the cloud I'd been riding high on had just crashed to the ground. I told Remy I would still help with legal matters and thanked her for being so understanding.

Eric and Steve got calls next, each sounding disheartened and a bit taken aback that I regarded seriously my dedication to Christ. I wished them well in the endeavor.

The label never materialized. I doubt the money came through. And in hindsight, I doubt the partnership would have worked. Steve had revealed himself to be difficult to work with, at times irrational and untrustworthy, and yet my paycheck, the stability of my household, would have been at his mercy. When I got through the disappointment, I saw the blessing. God had saved me from myself.

Chapter 9

The Crossroads

AT 11 YEARS OLD, I WITNESSED A SHOCKING HISTORICAL TALE OF dominance, cruelty, and pure evil. My mother permitted me—encouraged me—to stay up past my bedtime to watch the much-anticipated *Roots* miniseries, and each night I sat glued to the set, on the verge of tears. I saw whips, chains, and language unfit for dogs penetrating people's spirits. I saw parents torn away from children, husbands from wives. And I saw slave rape treated as a prerogative, not a crime.

I was horrified and carried my disgust to school each day for the length of the series and beyond. I didn't want to be bothered with white people, didn't want them telling me what to do, didn't want them teaching me a thing.

I knew about Jim Crow. My mother grew up as a share-cropper's daughter in North Carolina and told me about "colored" water fountains, segregated schools, and Negroes knowing their place. I had seen footage of the civil rights movement, of water hoses, billy clubs, and dogs unleashed on peaceful demonstrators. And I had been haunted by pictures of the Ku Klux Klan raising terror in the night. My opinion of whites had never been high, but *Roots* pushed me over the edge. Watching this country's low point live and in color had a profound affect on my psyche. White people, I concluded, were no good.

That feeling never left me entirely. From childhood into adulthood, I got along well with whites, met many whom I loved to death, but the white collective was not to be trusted. Laws, not good hearts, had forced them to be fair, and even still they found ways around "good," creating policies and standards favorable only to their own. Whips and chains were taken under cover, woven into institutional fabric, but African-Americans felt the sting nonetheless. We could be as talented and intelligent as we wanted to be but would be judged unworthy until we proved ourselves and then proved ourselves again and yet again.

To whites I was suspect, and they to me. I knew early on they wouldn't do me any favors—I wouldn't get the benefit of a good ol' boys network or old-school affirmative action (the whites-helping-whites kind). So I learned to play by their rules. I could talk the articulate talk, form good working relationships, do good work. I didn't wear braids, cornrows, dashikis, or other ethnic identifiers that could have made them uncomfortable. But even when I achieved their brand of success, I didn't sleep. I was in the game but would never be on the team. I'd never be one of them and didn't want to be.

I loved being black. Even when I fully understood past abuses and present discrimination, I didn't wish to be anything else. I liked my skin tone, the color white girls fried themselves to achieve. I liked the sense of family that abided in the African-American community. I liked black culture. And I liked causes, like the one that erupted my third year of law school.

Black male students couldn't seem to escape harassment. While waiting to enter a classroom, books in tow and surrounded by white students, a professor deemed one a "loiterer" and called security. Another black male was singled out when entering the library and asked to show his student I.D. as white students filed in ahead of him, uninterrupted. When he questioned the inequality, security filed a disorderly conduct charge, of which he was later cleared. And in a crowning incident, a black male was studying in the library when security forcibly arrested him for stealing a book bag, though he looked nothing like the suspect.

The Black Law Students Association, having witnessed these and other injustices mount, swung into action. After several office meetings and impromptu grievance sessions, we yielded a forum on race relations attended by the dean, faculty, and university administrators and covered by the *Washington Post*. I involved myself in every phase of strategy and also wrote an article for the school paper denouncing the harassment and highlighting my own negative treatment on the *Journal* staff. I enjoyed addressing wrongs, making white people stare at prejudices they pretended didn't exist. But more than that, I liked coalescing with my people, getting together with folk who felt the same pain, the same anger, and the same dignity and working toward a resolution.

I was black first. A woman second. But then I acquired this other defining adjective, *Christian*, and upset the status quo.

In the fall of 1995, the Million Man March grabbed headlines, first just a smattering and then, as the media awakened to the realness of the event, an almost daily barrage. With Louis Farrakhan at the helm, predictable reactions followed. A groundswell of support was building in the black community; skepticism and rancor reverberated in white and Jewish communities, where mere mention of the name "Farrakhan" made temperatures rise.

I enjoyed Farrakhan. In college and beyond I tuned in to his television interviews just to watch his trademark agility in handling the media. Hard-hitting interviewers would show up loaded for bear and go after him with documented statements, "evidence" of his allegedly racist and anti-Semitic tendencies. Unruffled, he'd deflect their barbs with eloquence and quiet assertiveness, often ruffling his accusers with pointed historical criticisms and charges of white conspiracies. I derived immense pleasure from watching a black man one-up the white establishment, showing intellectual prowess and remarkable cool while making no apologies for heavy-handed rhetoric. While I didn't buy into all of his claims, I considered him an asset to the black community, a man sure to keep his finger on the nation's racial pulse and alert us at the first sign of injustice.

I saw Farrakhan in action at the University of Maryland in March 1989, the year after I graduated. Security was tight. Officers abounded on horseback, on the roof of Ritchie Coliseum, and in a helicopter hovering above the building, and a security fence had been erected on the premises solely for his arrival. Farrakhan's own security, the Fruit of Islam, marched outside in tight formation like fraternity pledges. And an estimated 700 Jewish students protested vigorously. A group of sorors and I walked past them, and I rolled my eyes spontaneously, wanting to shout, "You all need to get a life. This is about black people dealing with 'family' business, trying to be uplifted and empowered. It's not about you."

Inside, Farrakhan was on fire, and he fired up a crowded auditorium with talk of black pride and the state of race relations in America. We cheered when he proclaimed that whites tolerate blacks when we're flying through the air with the greatest of ease, dunking a ball in a hoop, but not when we're in front of a classroom, teaching their kids. And when he echoed his familiar refrain about blacks deserving reparations for slavery, the crowd went wild.

Farrakhan had a way of engaging black people, speaking about ills we all observed, in words and tones other so-called black leaders dared not use in public. He had a flair for the provocative, and his conception and promotion of the Million Man March placed him squarely in his apparent comfort zone—out front, in the media, and in the middle of controversy.

I was amused by all the hullabaloo surrounding the march and definitely considered myself a supporter. The country would see black men united, taking care of business. I didn't care that women weren't invited; this was their thing, for the betterment of the black family.

St. Paul started a roundtable to discuss and formulate positions on issues affecting our city, nation, and world. Our first meeting was held on the third Sunday in September 1995. We met in the sanctuary that afternoon and began batting about current events when I raised the news of the day, the Million Man March. I had no idea the pastor would react as he did.

His head fell for a moment, and sorrow filled his voice as he lamented the support some Christians had voiced for the march. The pastor supported the stated purpose of the march and believed African-Americans needed to coalesce. His problem: The leader of the march was also the leader of the Nation of Islam.

I had always seen Farrakhan the black man, not Farrakhan the Muslim, chiefly because I didn't know much about Islam, other than the no-pork rule, the women-covered-up rule, and whatever I gleaned from *The Autobiography of Malcolm X.* Certainly, I had never focused on the Muslim view of Jesus Christ, or the views of any other non-Christian religion for that matter. If someone believed in "God," a higher power, I counted us on the same plane. But the pastor was about to set me straight. I could hear the lesson coming, and I sat up in the pew at full attention.

He said Christians believe in the Holy Trinity—the Father, the Son, and the Holy Spirit. We believe Jesus Christ is the Son of God, that He *is* God. Then he said that Muslims deny that Jesus is the Son of God. They say He was only a prophet, no higher than any other prophet. And that belief, said the pastor, separates us from them.

The pastor grew vehement. If we truly love Jesus, he said with pointed finger, we should be repulsed by the thought of subjecting ourselves to Muslim leadership, no matter what the cause. If we considered ourselves soldiers for Christ, we should have no room or desire to soldier for Farrakhan for even one hour. In the pastor's words, words that became the genesis of this book, "We need to be more Christian than Afro-American."

He preached, "Jesus doesn't care what color you are. Being black won't get you into heaven. It's how faithfully you follow Him that counts. Don't get caught up in this black stuff and lose your salvation."

The pastor regarded this issue very seriously and didn't want us to rely solely on his words about Islam; he wanted us to read it for ourselves. He brought the Koran to Sunday school the following week, with pages already copied and highlighted, which he passed out.

One passage read, "Such was Jesus, the son of Mary. That is the whole truth, which they still doubt. God forbid that He Himself should beget a son!"

Another referred to Jesus as a "servant of God" and a "prophet" and continued, "Those who say: 'The Lord of Mercy has begotten a son,' preach a monstrous falsehood, at which the very heavens might crack, the earth break asunder, and the mountains crumble to dust."

As one of "those" who believed the Lord begat a Son, I was indeed offended. In the year and three months since I had joined St. Paul, I had come to love Jesus, and the love grew stronger the more I studied His Word. How dare they minimize my God, my Jesus, I thought.

My spirit was on board with withdrawing support for the march, but my mind straddled the fence. It reasoned, "Okay, so Farrakhan doesn't believe in our God. But he's right on the money when it comes to race issues and what we need to do to uplift the community. Why *can't* I separate the message from the messenger?"

My spirit, eager to persuade, moved me to self-study. I opened the Bible Bill had given me as a gift and read Jesus' own words: "He who is not with me is against me" (Matt. 12:30).

And then I read from 2 John.

> Many deceivers, who do not acknowledge Jesus Christ as coming in the flesh, have gone out into the world. Any such person is the deceiver and the Antichrist. . . . If anyone comes to you and does not bring this teaching, do not take him into your house or welcome him. Anyone who welcomes him shares in his wicked work.

The force of the words shook me. Farrakhan not only didn't believe in Jesus; he was *against* Jesus, according to Jesus himself. And the warning from John not to welcome such a man. I thought, One million men answering Farrakhan's call. One million men trailing behind a man directly opposed to Christ. What a welcome wagon they will be for Farrakhan.

Still, I wrestled somewhat with my spirit. My mind justified, I've heard Farrakhan mention Jesus, and he didn't demean Him. Isn't this really just a black thing? Do we need to get caught up in religion for every little thing?

The spirit, fed up, turned cynical. Oh. Right. Farrakhan's gonna stand in front of all y'all black folk rooted in Christianity and dog Christ. That's a sure way to build a following. He's not stupid. He'll talk just enough about "God" to make you think he's with you, even throw you a bone a time or two and mention "Jesus," but he'll never tell you what he preaches in his mosque. What he *will* do is talk a whole lot about black issues to get you pumped up and on his team. But the Bible calls him what? A deceiver. Don't trip.

Race and religion had collided, both fighting for dominance, and only I could crown the victor. To be true to one meant a distancing from the other. I had pledged to walk with God, and my desire to do so was strong, but for the first time I realized the breadth of what that meant. Jesus was turning my life upside-down, infecting my perspective, causing me to question the soundness of my core.

The bottom line was my soul, my salvation. My goal was to be with Jesus in the end, not Farrakhan. So here on Earth I separated myself from Farrakhan and his march. I decided to become more Christian than African-American.

I didn't broadcast my opinion. Back home, friends and friends of friends were planning to take the subway downtown and join the masses. I kept my comments neutral and to a minimum—"Okay, let me know how it is"—and moved on. I was reluctant to admit my disapproval of the march for fear of being thought of as too religious. But one friend drew me out.

We were having lunch about one week before the march, and conversation centered first on the less-than-one-week-old verdict in the O. J. Simpson criminal trial. We shared similar views: He probably did it, but the bottom line was that the matter was between him and God; had the victim been black, we would not have been deluged with nonstop coverage; and wasn't it ironic that for years whites had gotten off for blatant killings of blacks and America hadn't cried "injustice"?

Parallels ended when he brought up the other "black" current event. He was headed to D.C. by plane, excited and full of talk about this march. He assumed I was supportive and engaged me in enough conversation that I had to speak up. I gave him an abbreviated version of my views, and he immediately interjected, contending the march had nothing to do with religion and Farrakhan was the only prominent person willing to do something about problems in the black community. I explained further, and he interjected further, until we had cultivated a full-blown, emotionally charged debate.

My friend believed in Jesus and considered himself a Christian but readily acknowledged his irregular church attendance and un-Christian lifestyle. I wanted to infuse all I had learned, all I had read, the insight given me by the Holy Spirit, so he would see my point of view. But all I had were my words and a few minutes of time, not nearly enough to turn him from a lifelong, pro-black course. I had lived in his spiritual place and wanted to bring him to mine, but he wasn't ready to be moved. I felt inadequate, like a lightbulb hung just above his head and I couldn't quite reach to turn it on for him.

That powerlessness came over me again with my father. Bill and I went home for Maryland's homecoming, a mere five days after the October 16 march. I expected to deal with march talk at Jasper's and at the campus tailgate, knowing that everyone who attended would be anxious to discuss it. But I didn't expect to encounter it at Daddy's.

We walked in the door fresh from our flight and saw two of my brothers walking around in "Million Man March" T-shirts with big Muslim symbols emblazoned underneath. I asked what was up with that, and Daddy informed me he had taken them downtown and how great an experience it had been. For a split second I thought about holding my tongue . . . *but my brothers were sporting Muslim paraphernalia.* I had to speak up, even realizing the uphill battle I was taking on. Daddy had fallen away from the church many years before, and we had never discussed anything Christian-related. He knew Bill and I had joined a church, though, and he was about to find out how serious we were about our faith.

I told him why the boys shouldn't wear Muslim gear and why, in my opinion, they shouldn't have been at the march. I talked about Farrakhan and Jesus, the whole deal. Bill even sprinkled in a comment or two. But my father wasn't with us. Aside from one concession—wondering why Nation of Islam literature had been placed along the march path—he took a turn in left field and began debating ways to enter into heaven and other major religious points. I grew more and more exasperated, my tone escalated, and my brothers and Bill looked highly uncomfortable.

I lost patience with Daddy, responding to one of his philosophical offerings with a cynical inquiry as to whether he had ever read the Bible. Bill met my eyes with a this-is-out-of-hand look, and I realized I had crossed the fair-debate line. I worked to introduce another subject, but when Bill and I left the house for a planned seafood dinner, I relived the episode on the way to the restaurant and all throughout the meal. I was concerned about my family's spiritual well-being and upset with the way I had handled myself. I wished I had spoken to Daddy one-on-one or at least walked away sooner rather than getting caught up in winning an argument.

As much as I desired to, I couldn't debate or argue Christ into Daddy's or my Midwest friend's hearts. Only they could do that. And I couldn't convince them of the truth. Only the Holy Spirit had convincing power. All I could do was plant the seeds, pray they be watered by God, and pray their hearts would be receptive when it happened.

As for myself, I prayed for strength and wisdom to walk the right way.

On the heels of the march, in December 1995, came another crossroads event: the *Waiting to Exhale* movie event. It was dubbed an "important movie," the black woman's "must-see." We had finally arrived. This was no piddling girlfriend-to-the-best-friend-of-the-main-character type of role. It was an all-black cast of leading ladies portraying successful middle-class women on the big screen. It was unheard of, and black women celebrated. *Exhale* parties sprang up across the country, including in Madison; girlfriends stood in long ticket lines and bought out theaters nationwide, propelling the movie to number one on opening weekend; and people talked and talked about this movie everyone had been waiting to see.

I had read the book years before and enjoyed it, even recommended it. I never questioned whether I would see the movie. I supported black directors and actors in lead roles and felt it my obligation to see their films on opening weekend, when ticket sales mean most.

But as I sat in the theater on *Exhale's* opening weekend, I knew I had changed. I wasn't the typical black woman, proud to see Whitney Houston, Angela Bassett, and others elevating our stock in Hollywood and showing America our stories are worth filming. I was a Christian, uncomfortable with the loose morals and profane language I had paid money to see.

This was an eye-opening period of self-examination and transformation, the most difficult adjustment I'd had to make on my Christian walk. I wasn't just putting aside a love of music; I was putting aside me. The pro-black me. The wrapped-in-blackness me.

It took some time to grow accustomed to my change of lens. Innate reactions had to be measured against Christian principles and suppressed when at odds. Politics presented a particular challenge. I had consistently and automatically discounted all things Republican. To me they were a stronghold of intolerance, anti-everything that wasn't white and male with an upper-class business suit. In their present-day ranks stood senators who fought hard to maintain segregation and less senior politicians whose platforms smacked of yesteryear. I wanted no part of them and couldn't fathom why any African-American would endorse their narrow agenda.

But when my new ears opened up, I heard the Republicans extolling "family values," denouncing abortion, and assailing the country's moral decline. I couldn't deny our affiliation of interests on certain issues and also couldn't deny that certain of my views had become "conservative." I disliked that word, *conservative*, and it made me cringe to try it on, but it fit. For the first time in my life, the Republicans and I had something in common.

But I still resented them. I still resented the white collective. And I knew my attitude didn't jibe with my faith. It certainly wasn't in line with my decision to be "more Christian." The march and the movie represented progress, but I was realizing my decision had far greater implications.

I had to figure out what it all meant, this elevation of my Christian self. Could I no longer be outraged at white people for their abominations? Would I have to love them no matter what? Even when *they* chose to be more white than Christian? And how would I release the hostility I'd been storing since childhood? How would I find room for forgiveness?

Unconditional love and forgiveness were two of Jesus' most basic teachings and two of the most difficult to implement. *I* chose who I wanted to love, and it was usually someone who loved me. Love meant "like," "caring," "do anything for you." And unconditional love was reserved for God, my parents, and Bill if he didn't act up.

Loving *everyone* required some deep Christianity. To love in the face of hate, discrimination, and foul play meant putting aside that spirit of vindictiveness I had so well nurtured. It meant not having to have the last mean-spirited word. It even meant not rolling my eyes in a show of loathing. I could dislike wrongdoing, even challenge it (God wouldn't have His children be doormats), but the stuff I had been harboring against white people didn't look, act, or feel anything like love.

Which brings me to forgiveness. I couldn't estimate how many times, with how many groups of African-Americans, I sat around and bashed white people for wrongs dating back hundreds of years. It was our right, our legacy, to hold tight to the resentment and stir it up whenever we good and well pleased. These were atrocities, after all, foul, low-down abuses that made us boil at their slightest retelling. The idea of laying them aside forever, casting away anger in favor of forgiveness, *never* entered my mind.

I had a hard time forgiving certain offenses, those that loomed beyond comprehension and notions of decency. It took a long while for me to forgive Daddy for keeping quiet about Bonita. I didn't love him any less or treat him with disdain, but in my heart sat this lump that reminded me every so often. When I'd think I had moved past it, the lump would swell up, and I would grieve all over again and lash out at Daddy in my mind. Only after I moved closer to Christ did I think seriously about forgiveness and about honoring my father. Daddy wasn't perfect, but neither was I. I released the bad feelings and found I enjoyed a heart freed up of dead space, space where Daddy's infraction had too long lived.

But Daddy's case was different. I loved him, and, comparatively speaking, his dead space had nothing on the mausoleum whites occupied in my heart. I couldn't extend the benevolence of forgiveness to a collective, people from whom I was emotionally distant but whose "crimes" had pierced my being. I had even thought about it once during a "love your enemies" lesson at church, but it wasn't in me. It just wasn't in me.

Then on January 15, 1996, in this period of "more Christian" transformation, I saw seven of the Little Rock Nine on *The Oprah Winfrey Show,* those brave souls who integrated Central High School in Little Rock, Arkansas, in 1957. They recounted their daily struggle against inhumane treatment, being beaten, kicked, and spat upon, and their remembrances ignited anger within me. After a commercial break, Oprah introduced three white adults in the front row, three of the harshest tormentors of the Little Rock Nine. I stared at them with contempt for their bigotry and malice, savoring a rare moment of fixation on actual oppressors. And unexpectedly, they apologized. Not a dry, clear-the-conscience apology but a remorseful, tears-about-to-surface apology. One approached the stage and hugged the seven. Tears flowed, and expressions of forgiveness rang forth.

I cried uncontrollably, awed by how warm these seven hearts were, while awakening to the hardness of my own. God had forgiven my sins and set my soul free, and yet I held the sins of whites captive, sins no more terrible in God's eyes than my own.

I let go. I used the tears to dredge up every hostile bone in my body and then just let it go. When my eyes dried and the redness cleared, I sat on my couch, staring into space, wondering what had happened.

The Spirit of God had filled me, strengthened me to accomplish the impossible. With God's help, race lost its grip over me, and Christ took hold.

Chapter 10

⋙◆⋘

Growing Pains

THERE WAS A WAY OUT OF MADISON. THE UNIVERSITY OF TEXAS AT Austin advertised an opening in mathematics education in the winter of 1996. Austin had for some time topped our list of desirable university towns, the list we compiled amid one of my early "I gotta get out of Madison" bouts. It had many pluses—weather, location near Bill's family in Dallas, a greater mix of people, Tex-Mex food, weather. I was sold without ever having seen the place.

Bill consulted me after reading the ad and inquired whether I still had an interest in leaving Madison.

"You're kidding, of course," I said. "When do we pack?"

"Smooch, don't think Texas is all wonderful. Austin is a beautiful city, but Texas is Texas. I encountered the worst racism of my life during my five years in Dallas. Rednecks are alive and well in Texas."

"Rednecks are everywhere. I'm not thinkin' about rednecks. I'm thinking about chillin' in my backyard in January, cooking chicken on the grill. I'm trying to live like *that*."

"I'm just making sure you know the whole deal before you get too starry-eyed. I'm trying to live like that, too. Let's go for it and see what happens."

Bill submitted his materials, and UT showed immediate interest. He flew down in mid-January, and I joined him one day later, leaving snow, ice, and subzero temperatures and deplaning to sunny, wonderful, 70-degree skies. My bones felt better. The air smelled sweeter. Happiness infused me with energy enough to do a lap around the parking facility, but I opted for a leisurely stroll to the rental-car booth. I was to drive to the hotel, where Bill would meet me after his day of being shuttled around campus and to dinner came to an end.

I couldn't wait to hear his impressions, whether he connected with the people, whether he even liked the people, whether I had something upon which to pin my hopes. But he hadn't returned by the time I arrived, so I ordered room service and read the local news to get a flavor for the city.

Much of the coverage centered around Barbara Jordan, who had died the day before. She taught politics, government, and ethics at UT's School of Public Affairs for 17 years, a position she assumed post-Congress, and the city seemed to hold her in high regard. I was only 12 when she left D.C., younger still when she served on the House Judiciary Committee that recommended President Nixon's impeachment. But the legend of Barbara Jordan had not escaped me. Like most trailblazers, she had been talked about enough over the years that I was well familiar with her firsts. In a weird way I was glad to be in her home state upon her passing to witness tributes paid to an accomplished American who happened to be black.

Bill returned feeling good about the day. His presentation had gone well—the graduate students in particular were enlivened by his discussion of race and math—and the faculty interviews had produced interesting discussions. His time with Ray Carrey, the gentleman leading the search for candidates, had been particularly noteworthy. Somehow, amid talk of mathematics reform and opportunity to learn, Christianity wove itself in, and they found they had a common bond in Christ. Bill said he could feel the meeting rise to another level, and I thought surely God was at work, placing His people in pivotal positions so His will might be accomplished.

Mr. Carrey picked Bill up Friday morning for more meetings, and I drove downtown and on campus to get a sense of the area. I had heard people refer to Austin as "the Madison of the south" due to its size and university center, but I noticed more differences than parallels. I saw far more Hispanics, Asian-Americans, and African-Americans. The buildings were taller, making Austin's downtown appear more cosmopolitan. And people seemed friendlier, perhaps a product of good old southern hospitality or good weather putting people in a good mood.

Bill's schedule of interviews ended Friday afternoon, so we were free to dine together, and we chose a Mexican restaurant recommended to us. Over an appetizer of tortilla chips and dip, we mulled over our future and assessed the likelihood of relocating to Austin. We verbalized many pros associated with such a move, but neither of us could come up with a con. One consideration in the forefront of our minds was the baby we were expecting. I was almost four months pregnant, and we preferred to raise our child in a more diverse environment, one in which he or she would be exposed to different cultures and not be the anomaly in classrooms and around the neighborhood. Austin didn't have the diversity of metropolitan D.C. or Chicago, where we were raised, but it was a few steps ahead of Madison. We agreed that if Bill got an offer and the terms were right, it would be very hard to refuse.

Prior to our arrival, Ray Carrey had arranged for his Realtor daughter, Lisa Barbour, to acquaint us with Austin's housing market. We wanted an idea of the cost of living, and I looked forward to seeing the style of homes native to the city. Early Saturday morning, Bill and I ventured out to breakfast, then headed over to Lisa's office. An attractive, somewhat petite, brown-haired woman greeted us with a warm Texas accent, sat us down, and told us what she had planned for our time together. She had reserved much of her day for us and thought we'd view cross sections of Austin's neighborhoods, sample Texas barbecue for lunch, and chat about Austin's highlights throughout. She was enthusiastic about serving as our tour guide and made it clear that Austin had much to offer.

Lisa showed us older homes within walking distance of campus, newer homes in south Austin, and still newer homes in Austin's hills. Bill, not one to cherish home shopping, fell in love with the hills and lingered in rooms with mountainous views. One community in the hills had a swimming pool and a private golf course for residents. In a fit of excitement, we vowed to build a home there, buy clubs, and take lessons so we could enjoy the full, picturesque vibe. We walked outdoors and stared silently at the vistas, sighing aloud and mentally transporting ourselves to the grounds on which we stood. In our minds we had made the move.

Lisa left us with maps, a relocation brochure, housing information, and assurances that we'd have at least one friend if we made Austin our home. The three of us had hit it off and had visions of her two kids one day baby-sitting for ours. We were careful not to get too far ahead of ourselves . . . but in weak moments I dared to dream.

UT called not a week later. They invited Bill to fly back down to meet the dean of the School of Education and gave indications that if the meeting went well, an offer would follow.

So I began my job search in earnest. I retrieved *Martindale-Hubbell* from my firm's law library and wrote down all the national law firms with offices in Austin, as well as the large Texas firms represented there. Then I called a law school buddy who worked in the D.C. office of one of these firms and obtained an Austin contact. I also contacted a woman I had met two years before in San Francisco at an American Bar

Association conference for women litigators. She worked in the Dallas office of a Texas-based firm, and, though I know she didn't remember me, she took the time to pass on my cover letter and résumé to the hiring partner in Austin. To the firms for which I had no contact, I simply sent résumés and letters detailing my interest, informing them of the dates I would be in Austin and expressing a desire to meet with them, if possible.

I had five interviews when we returned to Austin in February. While Bill spent his time on campus, I got acquainted with Austin's legal community. I didn't expect much diversity inside firm offices and, except for one standout, didn't find it. But I met people who seemed genuinely friendly and interested in meeting with me. I had gained a great deal of experience in my 4½ years at Michael, Best, more than most at my associate level, and a couple let it be known that their firms were in dire need of "qualified" minority attorneys. I, in turn, let them know, in the subtlest way possible, that I had several interviews and great interest in securing employment as soon as possible.

Bill and I didn't have time on this trip to look at homes or to see any other sights outside of downtown. We had just two full days, and, for both of us, they were crammed with meetings designed to secure our relocation. I called Lisa Barbour with news that we were back in town (which she'd heard already from her father) but unable to get together with her. She said she had additional communities for us to see and that we'd have plenty of time to find the perfect home in the spring. She seemed as excited as we that Bill had made it so far in the process. We both voiced a tinge of optimism that UT would come through.

That was my prayer, that Bill get an offer. And before we left Austin my prayer had been answered. The dean offered him a tenured position with a higher salary. And the following week, a firm I really liked invited me back for more interviews.

It was set. God's plan for us in Madison had been fulfilled—we had found Him again. As far as I was concerned, it was time to move on, taking God with us, of course.

I walked over to St. Paul from work one day for the noon worship service. We read scripture, Pastor Thomas gave a short sermon, and we ended with prayer and testimony. When others had left, I asked the pastor hypothetically what one should pray for if one were faced with an opportunity to move out of town. He said one should ask that God's will be done and that an appropriate prayer would be "Lord, please let me know in which city I can best serve you."

I walked back to work with a bit of the doldrums. The wording of the pastor's prayer demoted my own desires and placed God's first, which in theory was fitting but had the potential to undo all we had set in motion. Still, somewhat reluctantly, I incorporated this new request into my daily prayer and advised Bill to do the same. Not long thereafter, he got an answer I didn't like, that we needed to stay in Madison, at St. Paul.

I remember the day vividly. He called me at work with an "I've got bad news" sound in his voice. I closed my door and listened to him tell me he felt the Holy Spirit moving us to stay. He said that our work was not done, that he wasn't sure what lay ahead, but that we needed to stay a while longer at St. Paul. And he said the message was strong and clear, undeniable.

"Well, what if I feel just as strongly that God is directing us to go? You're not the only one who's been praying. You're not the only one guided by the Holy Spirit."

"Kim, can you honestly say God has spoken to you in that way?"

"I have felt all along that it was time to go. You said you did, too."

Bill spoke carefully. "But since we've prayed this new prayer, trying to discern God's will for us, have you felt strongly that we should go? Tell me and I'll listen, and we'll try to figure this thing out."

I had no honest comeback and wouldn't have been able to give it if I had. I was distraught, in tears, wanting to believe Bill had gotten his wires crossed but knowing deep down he hadn't. The minute the pastor recommended that prayer, my soul knew the tide was turning. It knew when we factored God into the equation, He would direct us as He saw fit, which wouldn't necessarily be as Bill and I saw fit.

But even as I swam in this realization, I expressed hurt to Bill for betraying our plans. He had turned on our hopes and dreams and reneged on his promise that we wouldn't be in Madison very long. Though the decision wasn't easy for him either, I made it all about me. Bill had put God's will before me, and the bottom line was that I didn't like it.

I wondered if I would ever get out. I wondered what God could possibly have left for us to do in Madison and why it couldn't be done somewhere else. I wanted to see His plan so I could understand why mine was being tossed aside. I could not fathom why God wouldn't favor this one request. "Why, Lord, can't I be blessed with warm weather and diversity?" I cried.

My blues lasted about a day and a half. I came to grips with the decision I knew in my heart was right and, by force of reality, readjusted my outlook. For five years I had been waiting for the day to leave Madison, and I wanted a peace to come over me. I wanted to stop complaining about living there (I had read umpteen times in the Bible about God's dislike for complaining) I wanted to stop focusing on what I didn't have and "be content whatever the circumstances" (Phil. 4:10). So I prayed for God to help me accept His will, to trust in His love for me and understand that He works only for the good.

As always, God answered.

Chapter 11

─══◆══─

I'm a Witness

IN THE SUMMER OF 1978, ONE YEAR AFTER DADDY AND JOYCE married, the three of us jumped in a car and headed south on I-95 for Spring Hope, North Carolina. I stretched out in the backseat and, for about four hours, alternated between sleep and singing along with Teddy Pendergrass on the eight-track.

Darkness had set in when we approached the Spring Hope exit. Daddy told me to pay attention, that if I blinked or sneezed, I might miss downtown. We passed storefronts reminiscent of Andy Griffith's Mayberry and turned up a gravel road to a house where people had cars parked every which way on the grass. Daddy fitted the Grand Prix into a makeshift space, and we got out and walked toward a crowd gathered outdoors, leaving our luggage for later retrieval.

The smell of fried fish pierced the warm country air, and music blasted as people clapped and stomped their feet. In front of them, center stage, were three girls: Sylvia and Yolanda, age 11, and Sheree, age 9. They were performing a dance routine to Teddy's "Get Up, Get Down, Get Funky, Get Loose" and had the crowd cheering. When the song ended, people yelled, "One more time," and the girls repeated their rehearsed steps.

I had met them at the wedding. Yolanda, Joyce's youngest sister, and I had served as flower girls. Sylvia and Sheree, Joyce's cousin and niece, had been guests. I couldn't remember the names of all the aunts and uncles milling about outside, though. Joyce had seven sisters and two brothers, and hers was only one of several immediate families represented.

When the crowd allowed the girls a break, they took me into the back room, into their inner circle, and taught me their routine. Later that night I shared their grassy stage and, by weekend's end, had felt the generous love of a large and wondrous group of people.

White America rarely hears about extended families in the black community like the Terrells. They uphold the institution of marriage, the rate of long-term marriages far surpassing incidents of divorce. They're steeped with college graduates—teachers, chemists, nurses, and business managers, to name a few—and promote the legacy with awards of scholarship money to high school graduates in the family. They're supportive, willing to travel hundreds of miles to celebrate birthdays, graduations, and weddings. And they're committed to a tradition of bringing their own together on the second weekend in August each and every year.

The Terrell family reunion is a big deal. Festivities kick off with an outdoor fish fry on Friday night, and, over the course of the weekend, folks count on steaks grilled to perfection and a pig roasted and chopped into delectable North Carolina barbecue. People play volleyball, bid whist in tournament rounds, football in the open field, basketball on Spring Hope courts, and, at least at Joyce's mother's house, stay up until five in the morning catching up on everybody's business. It's about bonding, sharing, laughing, rejuvenating, and packing into three days all the diversions one can stand. And, for me, it's been about hooking up with individuals I deem just as close as blood.

The Terrells embraced me from the start. They became my family. Through Daddy and Joyce's marriage, I gained a

Granny Morgan, an Aunt Sister Babe, an Uncle Opie, and dozens more affiliations. And, most dear to me, I gained cousins and confidantes in Yolanda, Sylvia, and Sheree.

They called us the Four Musketeers. Whenever we got together—at reunions, spring breaks, whenever—we journeyed around as if chained to one another's hips. Teenage summers offered ample opportunity. We spent weeks at a time at Sheree's home, in Neptune, New Jersey, taking trips to Great Adventure, the beach, the haunted mansion on the boardwalk, and the roller-skating rink. We spent weeks in North Carolina, rotating between Sylvia's home, in Raleigh, and Yolanda's, an hour away in Spring Hope, watching soap operas and walking to the country store for penny candy and dill pickles. We spent time in Maryland baby-sitting my baby brothers and looking forward to a Daddy-and-Joyce-sponsored trip to King's Dominion. And in whichever city we were based, we devoted time to perfecting a new dance routine.

We put on a show almost every year for my first few reunions, until we reached our late teens and began heading off to college. Carefree summers hanging out and rehearsing fell to the wayside; our child act became a "remember when." But as we retired, the family entertainment moved to another level. Someone suggested a talent show, and from then on we devoted Saturday evenings to watching a variety of acts from a variety of age levels. Over the years, some told jokes. Some lip-synched to a popular song. One juggled. But most danced, from one of my brothers' Michael Jackson imitation to the next generation of young girls doing their thing, to our cousins from New York breaking it down video-style. I sat happily in the audience, applauding, heckling, and whooping it up.

But in 1995, more than a decade after hanging up my dance shoes, I felt God moving me back out front, urging me to bring forth a spiritual message through song. And as anxious and out of my mind as such an endeavor would render me, I wanted to do it. I listened to one of the tapes I received from Brian Overton and heard music Remy and I hadn't used. Funky music. I listened on the way to work, and the chorus flowed.

> *Life can be hard to take*
> *Difficult decisions to make*
> *You can't take no more*
> *Put your faith in the Lord*
> *I don't worry about a thing*
> *All the trouble that life may bring*
> *I know He'll open up a door*
> *Put your faith in the Lord*

Then I wrote the verses, which spoke of hope and calling on Jesus when times get rough, and I shared my own testimony of finding Him and finding joy. Only earlier that summer I'd written lyrics for Remy, but I felt doubly excited writing for the Lord. I practiced it ad nauseam and told Joyce to add me to her list of talent show participants. But when the day came, I had an attack of misgivings.

I didn't know how the family would receive my song. Perhaps they preferred to hear about God on Sunday, not on Saturday night while beer flowed and a party atmosphere abided. And I didn't know how they would receive me, the new me. I had never confessed Christ publicly, outside of St. Paul, and wondered what reactions would follow. Perhaps some would think I was going through a phase, or I had become a bona fide religious lunatic. Either way, I wouldn't be cool. People would avoid me to avoid feeling self-conscious about what came out of their mouths.

But even as I fretted, God was at work. Just a couple of hours before the show, Joyce walked through her mother's house, rounded up the 20-something set, and asked us to sing a song at the show. We stared blankly at one another, and one, without any instigation from me, suggested a gospel song. We tested a few to see how well we knew the words and settled on the one everyone knew verbatim, Kirk Franklin's "The

Reason Why We Sing." We stood in a semicircle, with a young cousin playing Kirk's role, and practiced until harmonies blended.

Spring Hope's community center, less than one mile from the house, played host to our affair. After fried chicken, barbecue, coleslaw, potatoes, and greens, Joyce grabbed the microphone and hyped everybody up for the show they were about to see. The group gospel song preceded mine, and people got into it and sang along. I should have been relieved that the spiritual ice had been broken, and I was somewhat, but I figured their enthusiasm had more to do with the popularity of the song. Mine was new, fresh off the drawing pad. For it to go over well, they'd have to accept the music and the message. I was still nervous.

As the show proceeded all too rapidly, my stomach got more and more upset—combined jitters of singing alone in public and singing about Christ. I didn't hear my name when Joyce called it; I had run to the ladies' room to relieve some of the worry. When I returned, she asked if I was ready, and, halfheartedly, I said yes.

It was good that I liked the beat. When the groove started, I swayed my body from side to side and focused on a foot of space where no one sat or stood. A sea of burgundy Terrell reunion T-shirts packed the house, and I focused on none of them. I opened my mouth and started the chorus, but I doubt anyone heard the words. My voice said, "Yeah, you might have said you were ready, but nobody asked me."

I looked to God for help, and He pumped me with confidence. My voice grew louder and burst with more feeling. Ad-libs came out of nowhere. And the crowd, far from put off, started clapping to the beat. Heads nodded affirmatively, and when I sang my last "Put your faith in the Lord," I know I heard an "Amen."

Christie, the wife of a cousin, approached me after and introduced herself as a fellow believer. We had never taken the time to interact one-on-one at length, but meeting each other anew, as Christians, sparked a very special kinship. I would later learn of her commitment to living a righteous life, her devotion to studying God's Word, and her quiet wisdom, her ability to attach God-inspired power to soft-spoken words. She did it that night at the community center, looked me in the eye and told me, in her quiet, observational way, that God had redirected my boldness to a path productive for Him.

I dwelled on that simple message, on the evening as a whole, marveling at what God had done and who with. He had chosen me. *Me.* Still young in the faith. Tons to learn. But in His estimation, I had wings enough to fly, wings enough to carry my testimony from Wisconsin to North Carolina. I felt privileged to be used by God, like an awesome anointing had fallen upon my shoulders. . . . And I knew He had lots more for me to do.

For years, my mother slapped mortar between brick after brick after brick, stacking a divide tall and wide between herself and God. God bore responsibility for all the tribulations she suffered. On nights when her father seized the pittance she and her siblings had earned tending fields and used it to buy booze, returning home drunk and mean, God allowed it to happen. God allowed her to live in perpetual anxiety, forced to sleep lightly due to drunken rages and fear of not-too-distant harm. God heard her little-girl prayers but failed to answer.

God allowed her to marry Earl Cash at age 21, a man who truly loved her . . . but wasn't ready to settle down. She left six years later with a four-year-old in tow, trying to kick the dust of a failed marriage off her feet. Two males in her life, her father and her husband, had let her down—God had let her down—so she would fend for herself. She went to grad school at night, worked her way up the corporate ladder at AT&T, and settled into a comfortable, independent life. She didn't need support from anyone, not from a man, certainly not from the church, certainly not from God.

The church was full of ne'er-do-wells anyway, ministers pilfering from the collection plates and cheating on their wives. And God, well, whatever.

This is what Bill and I were up against. We heard it all, every justification for dodging organized religion and a relationship with God. Nevertheless, we wanted to bring her to Christ and tried every angle God put on our hearts. From the moment we joined St. Paul, we dropped casual conversation about the benefits of belonging to a church and our respect for Pastor Thomas. We let her see God working in our lives, how decisions were being made based on prayer and the guidance of the Holy Spirit. We testified to God's goodness when He blessed us. And we prayed diligently that she would see the light.

But as much of a witness as I endeavored to be, my patience ran low each time she doubled back to her upbringing. I understood and appreciated the gravity of the abuses but had heard the stories hundreds of times and knew they made up the bulk of that brick wall. I wanted her to let it go and stop blaming God. So when I heard her going there, sounding out that familiar refrain, I shut down. That's when Bill stepped in.

Bill and my mother would spend an hour on the phone and, on visits, sit up until well after I had gone to bed, talking about my mother's pain. She opened up to him about all she had been through, tears she had cried, prayers she had sent up, and the aftereffects that continued to plague her. She lamented over what she maybe could have been or done, given a saner childhood and a real marriage, forever living in the past, regretting and bemoaning. Patient Bill listened, went minutes at a time saying nothing but "Um-hmm." And when she was through, he would change the focus and point out the blessings.

"Yeah, I hear you, but despite your home life, you got straight A's in school and graduated with honors from college.

No, your marriage didn't work, but you got Kim, who you say is the biggest joy in your life. You had the wherewithal to raise her, educate her, and give her all the things you didn't have. You have a good job, make more money than most two-income families, live by yourself in a house with more room than most families. You have good health, a sound mind. . . . *Come on.* God has blessed you in a *big* way."

My mother, sobered momentarily, would acknowledge the truth of his statement. But down the road the dialogue would repeat itself.

One day, I cut to the chase. I told my mother that her soul was at stake, that heaven wasn't guaranteed to anyone, and that she needed to make changes before the hour grew late. She responded with a classic.

"I'm a good person. I don't hurt anyone, never broken the law. I'm generous to charities. I mail Momma a check each month. . . ."

I cut her off. "Ma, *'good people'* don't go to heaven. You have to accept Christ as your personal Savior and follow Him."

"What about all the other religions? Surely they think they've chosen the right path. How does one know who's right?"

"Jesus said, 'I am the way and the truth and the life. No one comes to the Father except through me.' We have to have faith and believe. It's not an intellectual exercise."

"I just don't know. And you're scaring me with this talk of heaven and hell. . . ."

"It's no joke, Ma. It is no joke."

As with Daddy, I realized my words would not be enough. Only God had power to break down that mighty wall. My mother needed to be moved by the Holy Spirit, shaken by the Holy Spirit. She needed spiritual convincing that Jesus loved her and had always been there for her, even as a child. She needed only to put aside herself, her logical, ever-rationalizing self, and believe. Bill and I prayed for that miracle, waited, then watched in amazement as it unfolded.

My pregnancy provided a huge catalyst. My mother knew our child would be raised in a Christian home and in a Christian church, and we made it clear that we wanted him or her surrounded by Christian role models. Wouldn't it be wonderful, we offered, if she could take part in that circle of Christian influence?

Something about the anticipation of a new life caused my mother to examine her own. She would be a grandmother, an important person in the child's life, expected to be wise, together, an exemplar. Yet she was incomplete, her spirit all but dead. For the first time, I heard longing in her voice, as if she wanted a place in the circle but didn't know how to position herself there.

We'd been advising she look for a church. She had relocated to Charleston, West Virginia, for a job promotion and wasn't familiar with places of worship. She resisted the effort, leaning for a good while on "the St. Paul excuse." Our church, which she visited on trips to Madison, was different. She felt unusually comfortable there, nothing like the awkward feelings she'd experienced at other churches in years past. And our pastor was upright, handing members reports of every check written on church accounts and keeping us apprised regularly of church business. And we had Marilyn Parks, a beam of radiant light to keep us uplifted and encouraged. Nothing in Charleston would stack up to St. Paul.

"Ma, I doubt you'll truly know if you just sit there on your couch. Ask around, and just go. You might have to visit a few before you find the right one. Just go."

Sigh. "Yeah, I probably should." No follow-through.

When I was seven months pregnant, in April 1996, a flyer appeared mysteriously in my mother's door, inviting her to a church service for Resurrection Day (a.k.a. Easter). She called immediately, sounding a tad out of breath, and told me what she had found.

"What does this mean? Do you think it means something?"

"Sure. God is answering prayer, making it easy for you to visit a church. You didn't want to get out and look for one, so the church came to you. You gonna go?"

"It *is* right up the street. I might just do it."

That night I launched into fervent prayer.

"Lord, please touch my mother's heart and mind, that she will be encouraged to follow through with this church visit. Then, Lord, please send the Holy Spirit with her into the church, that she will be moved by the service and overcome by your presence. Let her know, please, Lord, that you love her and that she belongs in your family. . . ."

God blessed Marilyn's daughter, Kendra, with a heavenly voice, one that makes you put down your church program, get your mind off the upcoming week, and focus. You feel what she sings. You close your eyes, lose all sense of time and place, and travel with her to the garden of Gethsemane or the little town of Bethlehem, the beauty of her voice outshone only by its message. She grew up singing for the Lord, and, unlike so many others, that's where she remains.

Kendra put together a Sunday school cantata for Resurrection Day '06. Preschoolers, grade-schoolers, teenagers, and adults retold Christ's last days on earth, and the choir sang the same in interludes from the loft. I had a solo, "Mary's Song," which placed me in the Virgin Mary's shoes. To sorrowful music, I sang about rocking and feeding my baby Son and watching Him take His first step, the same Son later crucified before my very eyes. As I sang Mary's pain, I reflected upon my own impending motherhood and the son I'd been told I was carrying. We had something in common, Mary and I. I could imagine more than ever her anguish and horror, simply based upon the love I felt already for my own unborn child. Jesus' death came to life again that day, and I mourned.

But as filled-up as the cantata and morning worship service made me, my mind drifted often to West Virginia. Had my mother gone, or was she sitting at home as usual?

I wasn't home 30 minutes when the phone rang. Not only had she gone; she had enjoyed the service. I praised God, told her how big and wonderful a step she had taken, and launched into even more fervent prayer when we hung up the phone.

"Dear Lord, my mother is at her most vulnerable. She's made movement toward you, and satan is not pleased. I pray that she be encouraged on this path and that satan be rebuked. Please, Lord, continue to move her in the right direction. . . ."

My mother called again that night. The pastor of the church had stopped by to see the visitor who filled out a card. She told him of the difficulty she had had making that step, and he ministered to her and prayed with her.

"Do you think this means something?" she asked. "I've never had a pastor visit me before."

I told her God was answering prayer once again.

My mother went to church the next week. Then the next. And she started going to Sunday school, too, much sooner than Bill and I did after we joined St. Paul. She called with lots of questions about the Christian faith, and we talked at length about the Bible. At times, in the middle of my own sentence, I would pause, look up, and mouth an expression of thanks to God. The once-impenetrable wall had fallen at His hands. She was seeking and walking, no longer challenging and debating. She would have much more to sort through, as with us all, but she had turned toward the light, and it was awesome. Awesome to have been used by God. Awesome to have a husband who loved her enough to help her along. Awesome to know that nothing is too hard for God.

My mother had never been baptized. Upon hearing this, I immediately suggested she have Pastor Thomas perform the ceremony so we could all take part and celebrate, including Marilyn and Bridget. They had been praying for her, and Marilyn had taken her on as a personal project, writing and calling to encourage her to come to God.

I had learned that baptism signifies the death and resurrection of Christ, burying the old way of life and coming into a new life with Christ. My mother was reborn on Sunday, July 7, 1996, in an emotional, Spirit-filled ceremony. And witnessing, albeit asleep, was her grandson, Quentin Emmanuel Tate, born June 28. We stood together as a family. She stood in the circle.

Chapter 12

Spiritual Junk Food

Like newborn babies, crave pure spiritual milk, so that by
it you may grow up in your salvation. (1 Pet. 2:2)

GANGSTA RAP CDS RESTED DEMURELY ON MY LIVING ROOM SHELF,
as did raps glorifying street-drug highs and nasty sex with
"hookers" and "hoes." The beats were so-o-o slammin' that I ignored the words for the sake of a serious groove.

R&B rested there, too, a lot of it as base as the rap, boldly
going where old-school Motown hits never traveled. "Let me
lick you up and down." "I wanna sex you up." "Come over and
let me do you all night." "Come over here and let me take off
your clothes . . . nobody has to know." Lust pervaded the
market. And I listened, caught up in catchy hooks, tempting
rhythms, and seductive vocals.

I watched the videos, males gyrating into close-up camera
angles and females jiggling half-naked bodies, including multi-
platinum artists who took well to skimping it up.

And I tuned in faithfully to favorite television shows that
promoted casual sex and spewed as many curse words as the
network would allow.

I came to Christ on a steady diet of spiritual junk food,

plates full of addictive fare but devoid of healthful substance. I craved it and digested it well, unaware of the cancer it had spawned within. The disease had been growing for years, trafficking through my soul, leaving it sullied and impure. It desensitized my mind to filth, distorted my view of acceptable versus unacceptable, and caused me to savor the unsavory.

My spirit knew well the damage I was inflicting and had, for some time, given me signs it needed real nourishment. But even after joining St. Paul, I didn't quite get it. I curbed my own language and behavior but consumed the foul language and behavior of others. My justifications: it was "downtime" in God's eyes, "harmless entertainment," just a song, just TV.

But my declarations were entirely self-serving. Part of me wanted still to be out there, enjoying the things I'd always enjoyed, maintaining a slice of the life I'd always lived. I didn't want to be uncool, clueless at Grammy time as to the artists and songs nominated in R&B and rap categories. So, despite what I believed to be true, I was half-in, half-out. One foot in the light. One foot in darkness. One eye on God. One eye on the world. One day a tall glass of spiritual milk. The next a heaping bowl of junk food.

Right around the time of my "more Christian" transformation, God's Word forced me to face facts. The more I studied, the more I ran across pointed commands. They blew up on the page and screamed for my attention.

> But just as he who called you is holy, so be holy in all you do; for it is written: "Be holy, because I am holy." (1 Pet. 1:15, 16)
> Come out from them and be separate, says the Lord. (2 Cor. 6:17)
> Do not conform any longer to the pattern of this world, but be transformed by the renewing of your mind. (Rom. 12:2)

And one just stared at me sweetly.

Whatever is true, whatever is noble, whatever is right, whatever is pure, whatever is lovely, whatever is ad-mirable—if anything is excellent or praiseworthy—think about such things. (Phil. 4:8)

Sometimes in my quiet moments of prayer and medita-tion, long after the stereo had powered down, I'd hear the words of the last songs I'd listened to. Prayers about living in the spirit would trail off as my mind chased sinful lyrics, none of them "pure," "right," or "true." But my mind had given them a home, and I couldn't kick them out even when I wanted to, not even in the middle of my one-on-one with God.

I realized I couldn't claim to be a living example for Christ while partaking in sin. Whether I fed it through my eyes or my ears, someone else's "stuff" entered my being and became my own. I needed to strive to get better, holier. I needed to separate from the things of the world and surround myself with things of God, things to keep me growing toward the light, as plants do, recognizing their source of everlasting life. I needed, simply, to become a "24-7" Christian.

As I filled up on spiritual nourishment, I lost my appetite for junk food. It became distasteful, unpalatable. I trashed cer-tain rap CDs and tapes (not all, 'cause not all rap is bad). A listening ban wasn't enough. I wanted the mess out of my house. I began screening R&B music, listening only to songs that passed lyrical muster. And I stopped making a meal out of music videos, instead sampling only now and then, with the remote in hand so I could flip when things turned foul.

I nixed favorite television shows and limited my viewing to "news magazines" and shows like *Law and Order* and *Cosby*. I chose carefully my trips to the theater (especially after *Waiting to Exhale*) and routinely turned away from cable movies in mid-film, because I couldn't take another "g—d—." I cut off my favorite soap opera after 15 years of viewership, giving in to the nagging realization that, fiction or not, I had to stop filling up on trash. And I canceled my subscription to a hip music-industry magazine for writing countless articles with vulgar language and lurid sex talk and, the final straw, sending what might as well have been a *Playboy* cover to my home.

But change didn't come overnight. Now and then I gave in to Temptation when it insisted, "It's not that bad. Go ahead and partake." I'd pop in a tape that I'd sworn off just to hear a beautiful vocal arrangement. And sometimes I'd ease into the bookstore and flip through the offending magazine to see who was hot, who was dating whom, and who was suing what label.

Bill wasn't much help on the music end of the transition. He couldn't identify with my struggle. He had never shared my love for music or the music industry and had told me long before to "turn off those raunchy videos." But Bridget was there. She, too, had been a fan of hip-hop and R&B and, like me, was striving to better her diet. We leaned on Christian support, pumping up the new life to which we were committed and encouraging each other not to step back in time. Neither of us gave up the secular totally, but we became an advisory board for each other, placing our stamp of approval on albums like Babyface's *The Day* and Boyz II Men's *Evolution* and, with regard to most others, calling to say, "Don't even buy that, girl."

Bridget also pushed me to ax a television show I hadn't quite given up. I knew it was over the top, even acknowledged it, but every Thursday the plots pulled me in. One night, in the middle of the show, the phone rang. I knew who it was.

"Girl, did you hear that dialogue?! Calling her a b—— and talking about kicking her a—! They've been cursing every two minutes. And you see who they're about to start an affair with, don't you? They always got to go to the bedroom. This is just trash. I'm done."

". . . Yeah . . . I did notice all that. I know. You're right. . . . But . . . I just want to see what's going to happen. You know it'll get good over the next few weeks. But you're right. I need to cut if off."

Overcome by guilt, I did.

As the wedge between myself and the world grew bigger, my taste for the spiritual intensified. I devoured the Word, especially letters from Paul, Timothy, Peter, and James in the New Testament. Filled with blunt instructions for Christian living, they affirmed my path and strengthened me to keep on task.

I also turned to gospel music. I had never bought a straight-up "Praise the Lord" CD. Gospel was for church. R&B for car and home. But I heard Kirk Franklin on the radio in Chicago one day, and it blew my mind. I thought, Jesus? On the radio in the middle of the workweek?

Kirk put praise to modern beats, and I ate it up, buying album after album released with his songwriting touch. (The self-titled album, *Kirk Franklin and the Family*, *Whatcha Lookin' 4*, the *Kirk Franklin and the Family Christmas Album*, *God's Property*, and *The Nu Nation Project*.) I could groove to the music and at the same time nourish my soul. He came strong in the name of Jesus, never copping out with ambiguous references to "He," a "higher power," or "the Creator." And he came biblically correct, too, often lifting verses verbatim and sprinkling them through his music.

I got so I listened to Kirk Franklin in my office with the headphones, while working out at home on the treadmill, even on road trips to Milwaukee and Chicago when I could have tuned in to black radio. I'd shoot down the highway with one hand raised in holy agreement, laughing out loud in joy, rocking and singing, filled up with the Holy Spirit and enjoying a good time in the Lord. When I reached that mountaintop, the last thing I wanted to hear was R&B.

I caught the Stellar Gospel Music Awards show the year Kirk Franklin received "Song of the Year" honors for "Stomp," a song that used rap and a George Clinton sample to bring Jesus to the young, hip-hop crowd. He took the mike in a reflective, cheerless state and said the song's contemporary style had caused people to question whether God was really in what he was doing. He said it hurt.

I wanted to tell him, "My brother in Christ, you've given me songs to sing, righteous lyrics I can house in memory and retrieve at will. You put Jesus in places He hadn't been, in my speakers and at the heart of my so-called 'downtime.' My soul cheers when we dine at your table; like a waterfall, your words rush forth with each swallow and choke its impurities, giving it strength and renewed vitality. Your messages have pulled me through storms, funks, and embattled workdays, times I could just close the door on the world and put on Jesus through song.

"You keep on keepin' on, my brother. I thank God for you."

Chapter 13

Onward and Upward

IN JANUARY 1997, ONE YEAR AFTER WE DECLINED UT AUSTIN'S offer, the school was back on the radar screen. They hadn't given up on Bill and sought to recruit him and another woman to recharge their mathematics education program. Willing to see where this round might lead, he flew down to meet with them again, but I stayed home with Quentin, partly because traveling with a seven-month-old is cumbersome but mostly because I had no desire to board that roller coaster again. I didn't want to feel the balmy breezes, didn't want to see the scenic homes, didn't even want to see Lisa Barbour.

I had finally, miraculously, reached a point of satisfaction about living in Madison. I had stopped complaining. I made the most of the beautiful summer weather. I even rooted for the Super Bowl–bound Green Bay Packers.

And the thought of leaving Bridget and Marilyn saddened me. For two years, the Christian Women's group had been as important a part of my life as bread and butter. Every week I looked forward to studying the next Old Testament chapter, getting feedback on personal issues, sharing testimonies of God's goodness, and receiving prayer for special concerns. So many prayers had gone up in that group, and every one had been answered. Every one.

I had grown by leaps and bounds as a result of Marilyn's guidance and fervent encouragement. She had helped prepare me to leave her nest, but I wasn't ready to go. I had firsthand knowledge of the power of a good Christian support network, and the thought of finding another as mighty as that one was less than appealing.

So I didn't get emotionally vested this time around. I didn't pray for Bill to get an offer. I prayed that God's will would be revealed as it was before and that we would follow His will, whatever it might be.

The process moved along quickly, and Bill grew more and more excited over the possibilities. He and the other woman, whom Bill had known for some time, talked about grants they could pursue and assistant professors they could add to the program. Bill believed they could increase the school's profile in math education and truly make a contribution. And so, apparently, did UT. They offered him another tenured position, this time with more perks and a higher salary, enough for me to take time off from my career and care for our son full-time.

I so wanted to do that. Motherhood had been a far greater joy than I'd ever imagined. I simply stared sometimes at the precious gift God had given us and marveled at His goodness. I thanked Him daily for Quentin and for bringing forth in me more love, selflessness, patience, and energy than I'd ever before mustered. I so valued my time with Quentin that I reduced my schedule to part-time one month after returning from maternity leave. But, surprisingly, my heart's desire was to leave entirely for a while, no matter what the consequences. And UT was giving me a chance to do that.

Why, we wondered, would the opportunity arise again, and in more attractive form, if we weren't meant to grab it? It seemed to make sense that now was the time to go, that we were being blessed with this better package as a reward for listening to God the first time, and now He was sanctioning the move. My insides churned in suppressed excitement as I made tentative plans. I would call Lisa to find out what we could afford on one salary. We'd have to start looking for a new church home. Maybe my mother could retire and join us in Austin . . . she liked warm weather.

But the unexpected happened again. One day after church, we were sitting in The Original Pancake House, our favorite breakfast place in Madison. Bill obviously had something on his mind, and I was trying to pull it out of him.

"Well," he said, "for the last couple of days I've had this weird feeling. I feel like God is calling me to preach. It's like . . . no doubt in my mind."

At that moment, I knew we had our answer. Bill had a bird in hand in Madison, a serious pastor under whose leadership and teaching we had already grown tremendously. That he should stay and train under him was a no-brainer.

That week, we visited Pastor Thomas together and told him of Bill's calling. The pastor announced matter-of-factly that he had had a vision months before that Bill would come to him with this very news, and Bill and I stared at each other in disbelief. We had confirmation. There truly was more for us to do in Madison.

Bill turned down UT Austin once again, and that very semester he received tenure from the University of Wisconsin—one year early—and a hefty pay increase. We thanked and praised God.

I reflected on my turnaround about living in Madison, and the wondrous nature of God rang forth. Six years before, when I had cried and stressed myself out about moving to Madison, He had a plan. When I hadn't found a permanent job yet in D.C. but was offered the perfect job in Madison, He had a plan. When I complained about the whiteness, the weather, and the everything else I found wrong with Madison,

He had a plan. And when He put Bill in my path and kept us bound together in times of trial, He had a plan.

I wasn't "God-forsaken," or serving some horrific sentence, as I had once concluded. God had rescued me, lifted me from the depths of darkness, and brought me to Him. And He blessed me with a mate willing to grow in Christ, one with whom I can share in the journey and on whom I can lean when the road gets rocky. Had we stayed in D.C., we would have remained in diversity, but given the course we were on, we might have also remained utterly lost. I finally got it. I finally understood.